Math in F⊙cus®

Singapore Math®
by Marshall Cavendish

Student Edition

Program Consultant
Dr. Fong Ho Kheong

Author
Michelle Choo

U.S. Consultant
Susan Resnick

Marshall Cavendish
Education

U.S. Distributor

Houghton Mifflin Harcourt.
The Learning Company™

Grade
KA

Contents

Chapter

1 Numbers to 5

Chapter Opener   1

1 All About 1 and 2	**2**
All about numbers 1 and 2	2–6
PRACTICE	7
2 All About 3 and 4	**11**
All about numbers 3 and 4	11–18
PRACTICE	19
3 All About 5	**21**
All about number 5	21–24
PRACTICE	25

© 2020 Marshall Cavendish Education Pte Ltd

4 All About 0	**29**
All about number 0	29–32
PRACTICE	33

5 Order Numbers to 5	**35**
Order	35–37
GAME	38
PRACTICE	39

PUT ON YOUR THINKING CAP!   **41**

MY MATH DICTIONARY   **42**

CHAPTER REVIEW   **43**

PERFORMANCE TASK   **47**

© 2020 Marshall Cavendish Education Pte Ltd

2 Numbers to 10

Chapter Opener   49

1 All About 6 and 7	**50**
All about number 6	50–55
All about number 7	56–60
PRACTICE	61
2 All About 8 and 9	**65**
All about number 8	65–70
All about number 9	71–76
PRACTICE	77
3 All About 10	**81**
All about number 10	81–86
PRACTICE	87
4 Order Numbers to 10	**89**
Order	89–90
PRACTICE	91

© 2020 Marshall Cavendish Education Pte Ltd

5 **Make Number Pairs to 10**	**93**
Make number pairs of 2, 3, 4, and 5	93–97
Make number pairs of 6 and 7	98–100
Make number pairs of 8 and 9	101–103
Make number pairs of 10	104–106
PRACTICE	107
6 **Ordinal Numbers**	**109**
Use ordinals to tell order	109–111
GAME	112
PRACTICE	113

PUT ON YOUR THINKING CAP!	**115**
MY MATH DICTIONARY	**117**
CHAPTER REVIEW	**119**
PERFORMANCE TASK	**123**

© 2020 Marshall Cavendish Education Pte Ltd

Chapter

3 Measurement

Chapter Opener   **125**

1	**Compare Lengths**	**126**
	Compare the lengths of two objects	126–131
	Measure length	132–136
	PRACTICE	137
2	**Compare Heights**	**141**
	Compare the heights of two objects	141–146
	Measure height	147–150
	PRACTICE	151

© 2020 Marshall Cavendish Education Pte Ltd

3 Compare Lengths, Heights, and Weights — **155**
Compare the weights of two objects — 155–158
Compare lengths, heights, and weights — 159–163
GAME — 164
PRACTICE — 165

PUT ON YOUR THINKING CAP! — **171**

MY MATH DICTIONARY — **173**

CHAPTER REVIEW — **175**

PERFORMANCE TASK — **181**

© 2020 Marshall Cavendish Education Pte Ltd

4 Compare Numbers to 10

Chapter Opener — **183**

1 **More Than**	**184**
Compare using more than	184–188
PRACTICE	189
2 **Fewer Than**	**191**
Compare using fewer than	191–196
PRACTICE	197
3 **Same**	**199**
Compare using the same	199–202
PRACTICE	203

© 2020 Marshall Cavendish Education Pte Ltd

4 Compare Numbers to 10   **205**

Compare two numbers using greater than,   205–208
less than, and the same

Use 1 more and 1 less   209–213

GAME   214

PRACTICE   215

PUT ON YOUR THINKING CAP!   **219**

MY MATH DICTIONARY   **221**

CHAPTER REVIEW   **223**

PERFORMANCE TASK   **227**

© 2020 Marshall Cavendish Education Pte Ltd

5 Flat and Solid Shapes

Chapter Opener

231

1 Flat Shapes	**232**
Name flat shapes	233–235
See flat shapes around us	236–238
PRACTICE	239
2 Solid Shapes	**241**
Name solid shapes	241–243
See solid shapes around us	244–245
Roll, slide, and stack	246–248
PRACTICE	249
3 Positions	**253**
Use position words	253–256
PRACTICE	257
4 Make New Shapes	**259**
Use flat shapes to make new shapes	259–261
Cut flat shapes to make new shapes	262–265
Make pictures with flat shapes	266–268
Build solid shapes	269–270
PRACTICE	271

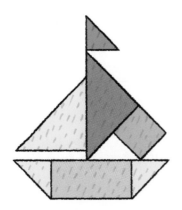

© 2020 Marshall Cavendish Education Pte Ltd

5 Compare Flat and Solid Shapes   **275**
Compare flat shapes   275–279
Compare solid shapes   280–282
PRACTICE   283

6 Shape Patterns   **285**
Use shapes to look for patterns   285–287
GAME   288
PRACTICE   289

PUT ON YOUR THINKING CAP!   **291**

MY MATH DICTIONARY   **292**

CHAPTER REVIEW   **295**

PERFORMANCE TASK   **303**

© 2020 Marshall Cavendish Education Pte Ltd

Glossary   **307**

Photo Credits   **317**

Manipulative List

Attribute block tray

Geometric solids

Connecting cubes

Spinner

Transparent counters

© 2020 Marshall Cavendish Education Pte Ltd

Preface

Welcome to **Math in F⊙cus**®!
We are the mascots.
Let us learn math with you!

© 2020 Marshall Cavendish Education Pte Ltd

Let us explore this book together!

Each chapter starts with pictures!
I can see how math is all around us.

This is what you will do in each chapter.

You will **LEARN** new math with your classmates.

You will **TRY** questions with help from your teacher.

You will **PRACTICE** questions on your own.

You will play a **GAME** and have fun with math.

You will **PUT ON YOUR THINKING CAP!** to answer some problems which are a little harder.

You will see the new words you have learned in **MY MATH DICTIONARY**.

You will think back on what you learned in the chapter in the **CHAPTER REVIEW**.

You will show what you know by working on the **PERFORMANCE TASK**.

© 2020 Marshall Cavendish Education Pte Ltd

Numbers to 5

0	1	2	3	4	5
zero	one	two	three	four	five

© 2020 Marshall Cavendish Education Pte Ltd

1 All About 1 and 2

LEARN All about numbers 1 and 2

© 2020 Marshall Cavendish Education Pte Ltd

TRY

Match.

Count.
Show how you count.

2

3

© 2020 Marshall Cavendish Education Pte Ltd

Trace each number.

Count.
Write each number.

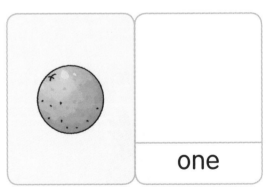

one

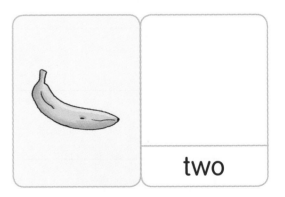

two

© 2020 Marshall Cavendish Education Pte Ltd

Count and match.

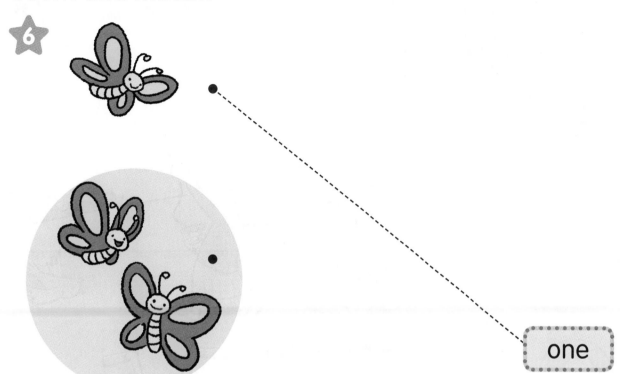

one

two

© 2020 Marshall Cavendish Education Pte Ltd

Circle the groups of 2.

© 2020 Marshall Cavendish Education Pte Ltd

PRACTICE

Match.

  ● ●

 ● ●

Count.
Color to show how many.

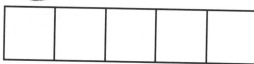

© 2020 Marshall Cavendish Education Pte Ltd

Draw.
Write each number.

 3 Draw **one** door.

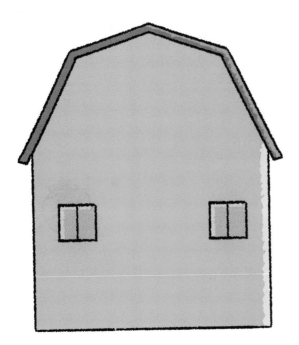

one

 4 Draw **two** doors.

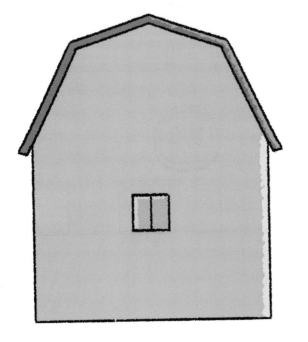

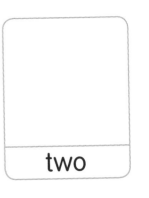

two

© 2020 Marshall Cavendish Education Pte Ltd

Draw one ◯.

5

Draw two △.

6

© 2020 Marshall Cavendish Education Pte Ltd

Circle the groups of 2.

7

© 2020 Marshall Cavendish Education Pte Ltd

2 All About 3 and 4

LEARN All about numbers 3 and 4

One, two, three, four.
Ants are crawling on the floor.
One, two, three, and four.
I like counting even more.

© 2020 Marshall Cavendish Education Pte Ltd

Match.

 • •

 • •

• •

 • •

© 2020 Marshall Cavendish Education Pte Ltd

Count.
Show how you count.

 2

 3

 4

 5

© 2020 Marshall Cavendish Education Pte Ltd

Count.
Color to show how many.

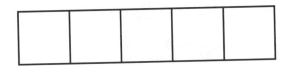

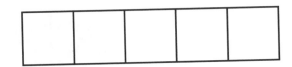

Trace each number.

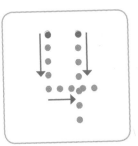      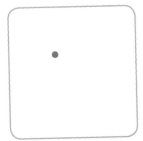

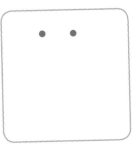 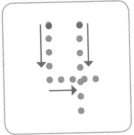

© 2020 Marshall Cavendish Education Pte Ltd

Count.
Write each number.

  9

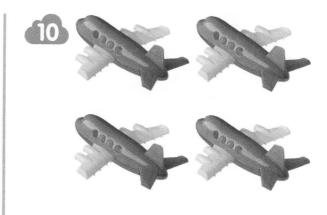 10

  11

 12

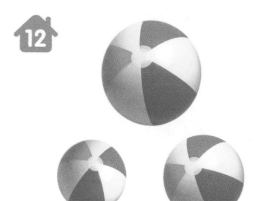

© 2020 Marshall Cavendish Education Pte Ltd

Count and match.

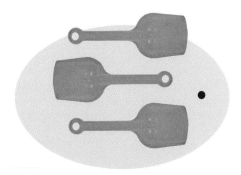

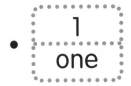

1
one

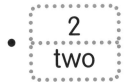

2
two

3
three

4
four

© 2020 Marshall Cavendish Education Pte Ltd

Print the correct number of next to each .

© 2020 Marshall Cavendish Education Pte Ltd

Use ⬤ to make a story about 3 and 4.

15

© 2020 Marshall Cavendish Education Pte Ltd

PRACTICE

Match.

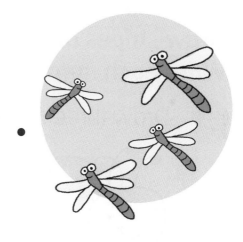

© 2020 Marshall Cavendish Education Pte Ltd

Count.
Color to show how many.

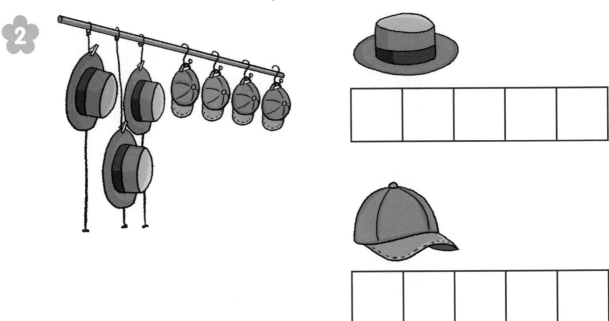

Draw stripes on each bee.
Write each number.

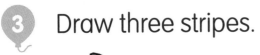

3 Draw three stripes.

three

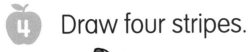

4 Draw four stripes.

four

© 2020 Marshall Cavendish Education Pte Ltd

3 All About 5

LEARN All about number 5

© 2020 Marshall Cavendish Education Pte Ltd

TRY

Match.

 1

© 2020 Marshall Cavendish Education Pte Ltd

Count.
Color to show how many.

 2

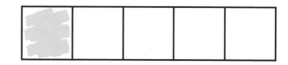

 3

 4

 5

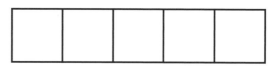

 6

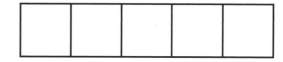

© 2020 Marshall Cavendish Education Pte Ltd

Trace each number.

five

Count.
Write each number.

© 2020 Marshall Cavendish Education Pte Ltd

PRACTICE

Match.

   •   •

   •   •

   •   •

   •   •

   •   •

© 2020 Marshall Cavendish Education Pte Ltd

Count.
Write each number.

© 2020 Marshall Cavendish Education Pte Ltd

Circle the groups of 5.

© 2020 Marshall Cavendish Education Pte Ltd

Draw  to show five.
Write each number.

4

five

5

five

© 2020 Marshall Cavendish Education Pte Ltd

4 All About 0

LEARN All about number 0

© 2020 Marshall Cavendish Education Pte Ltd

TRY

Match.

   •

   •

   •

   •

   •

   •

   •

   •

© 2020 Marshall Cavendish Education Pte Ltd

Trace.
Write each number.

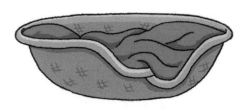  

© 2020 Marshall Cavendish Education Pte Ltd

Count the balloons.
Write each number.

© 2020 Marshall Cavendish Education Pte Ltd

Name: _____ Date: _____

PRACTICE

Count.
Write each number.

 1

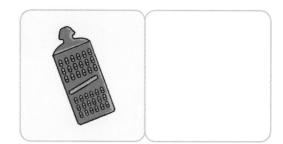

© 2020 Marshall Cavendish Education Pte Ltd

Match each nest to the correct box.

2	3
two	three

1
one

4
four

0
zero

5
five

© 2020 Marshall Cavendish Education Pte Ltd

5 Order Numbers to 5

LEARN Order

© 2020 Marshall Cavendish Education Pte Ltd

Count.
Write each number.

© 2020 Marshall Cavendish Education Pte Ltd

Write each missing number.

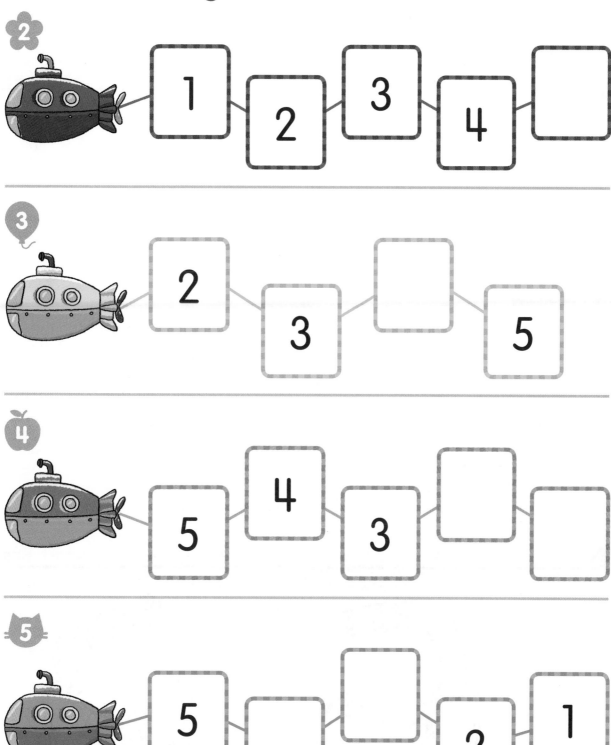

2 1 2 3 4 ☐

3 2 3 ☐ 5

4 5 4 3 ☐ ☐

5 5 ☐ ☐ 2 1

© 2020 Marshall Cavendish Education Pte Ltd

BINGO

What you need:

Players: 4 – 6
Materials: 2 bingo cards, game cards, a bag

What to do:

Put the game cards in the bag.

1 Player 1 picks a card from the bag. Count the number of objects on the card. Then, make an ✗ on that number on your bingo card.
If your number was already crossed, it is your partner's turn.

2 Trade places. Repeat 1 .

Who is the winner?

The player who crosses out five numbers on his or her bingo card first wins.

© 2020 Marshall Cavendish Education Pte Ltd

PRACTICE

Trace each number.
Color to show the number.

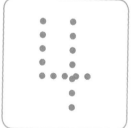

© 2020 Marshall Cavendish Education Pte Ltd

Connect the dots in order.

2

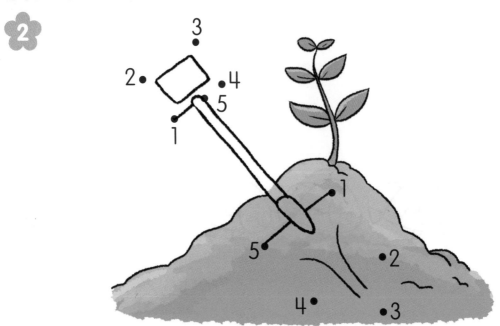

Write each missing number.

3

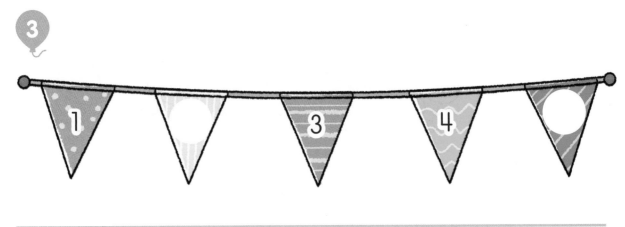

4

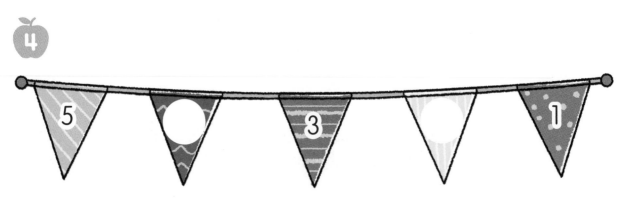

© 2020 Marshall Cavendish Education Pte Ltd

Name: _____

Date: _____

1 Circle the group with 3 .

Draw two other ways to show 3 .

2 Bella counts the seashells.

0, 1, 2, 3
There are 3 seashells.

Is she right?
How many seashells are there?
Count them.
Fill in the blank.

There are _____ seashells.

© 2020 Marshall Cavendish Education Pte Ltd

MY MATH DICTIONARY

1 one

2 two

3 three

4 four

5 five

0 zero

© 2020 Marshall Cavendish Education Pte Ltd

Name: _____   Date: _____

Count and match.

   •   •

   •   •

   •   •

   •   •

     •   •

© 2020 Marshall Cavendish Education Pte Ltd

Count and match.

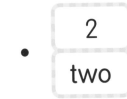

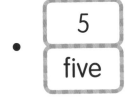

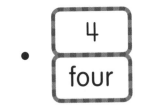

| 1 |
| one |

| 2 |
| two |

| 5 |
| five |

| 3 |
| three |

| 4 |
| four |

© 2020 Marshall Cavendish Education Pte Ltd

Count.
Write each number.

Write each missing number.

© 2020 Marshall Cavendish Education Pte Ltd

Assessment Prep
Answer each question.

 Circle the groups that show 5.

 Count the balloons.

Circle all the boxes that tell how many.

zero	3
four	4

© 2020 Marshall Cavendish Education Pte Ltd

Name: _____ Date: _____

Time for a Picnic

 1 Isabel brings 3 balloons to a picnic.

a Draw ◯ to show the number of balloons.

b How many balloons does Isabel bring?
Circle the correct word.

two · · · three · · · four

---

 2 Tomas makes five pies.

a Draw ◯ to show the number of pies.

b How many pies does Tomas make?

© 2020 Marshall Cavendish Education Pte Ltd

Count.
Write each number.

© 2020 Marshall Cavendish Education Pte Ltd

6	7	8	9	10
six	seven	ei ht	nine	ten

© 2020 Marshall Cavendish Education Pte Ltd

Name: _____ Date: _____

1 All About 6 and 7

LEARN All about number 6

TRY

Match.

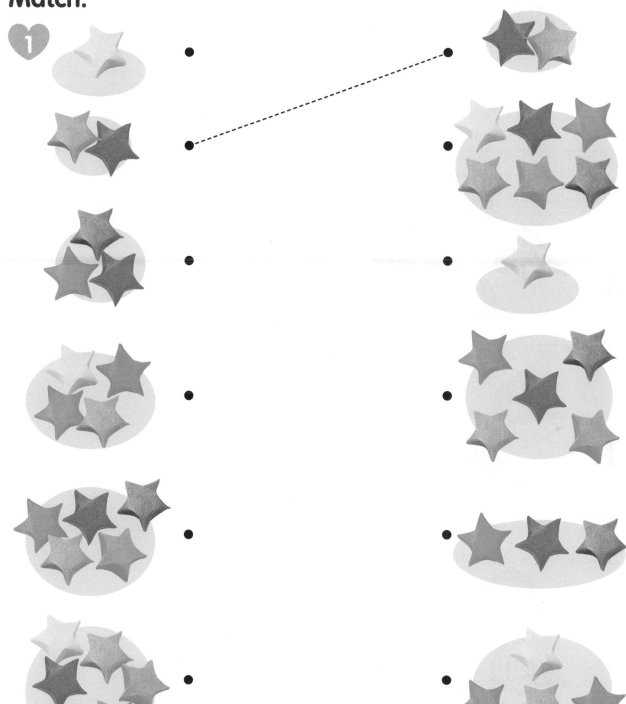

© 2020 Marshall Cavendish Education Pte Ltd

Count.
Use  to show how you count.

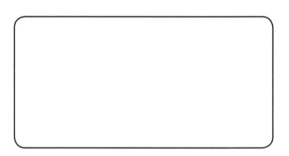

© 2020 Marshall Cavendish Education Pte Ltd

Trace each number.

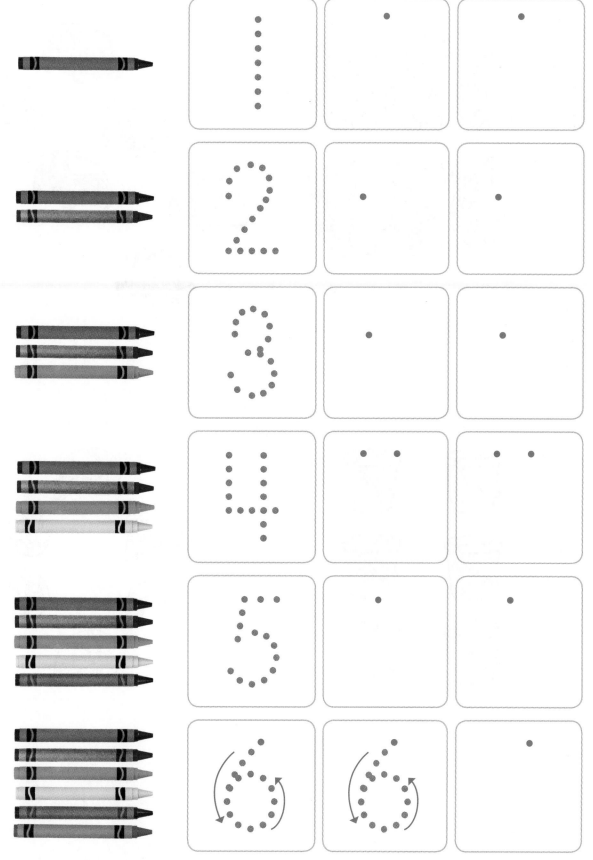

© 2020 Marshall Cavendish Education Pte Ltd

Count.
Write each number.

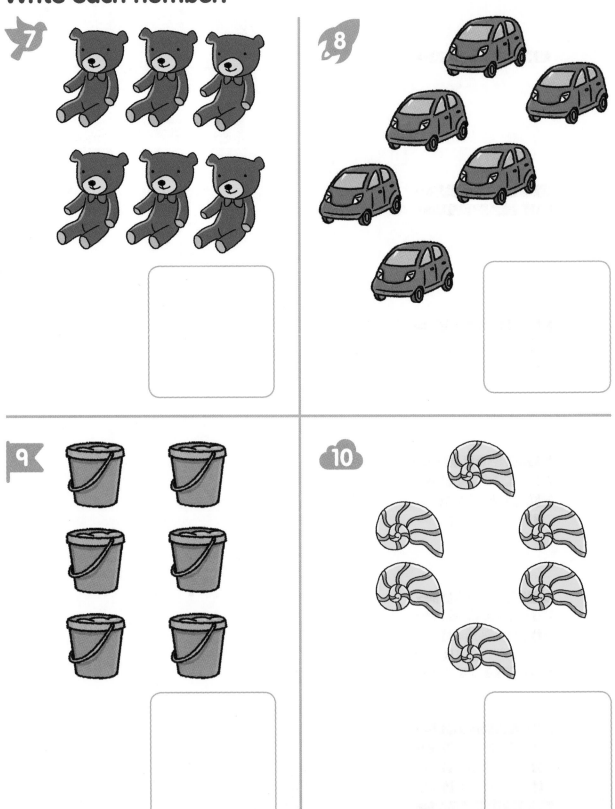

© 2020 Marshall Cavendish Education Pte Ltd

Draw six spots on the **.**
Write the number.

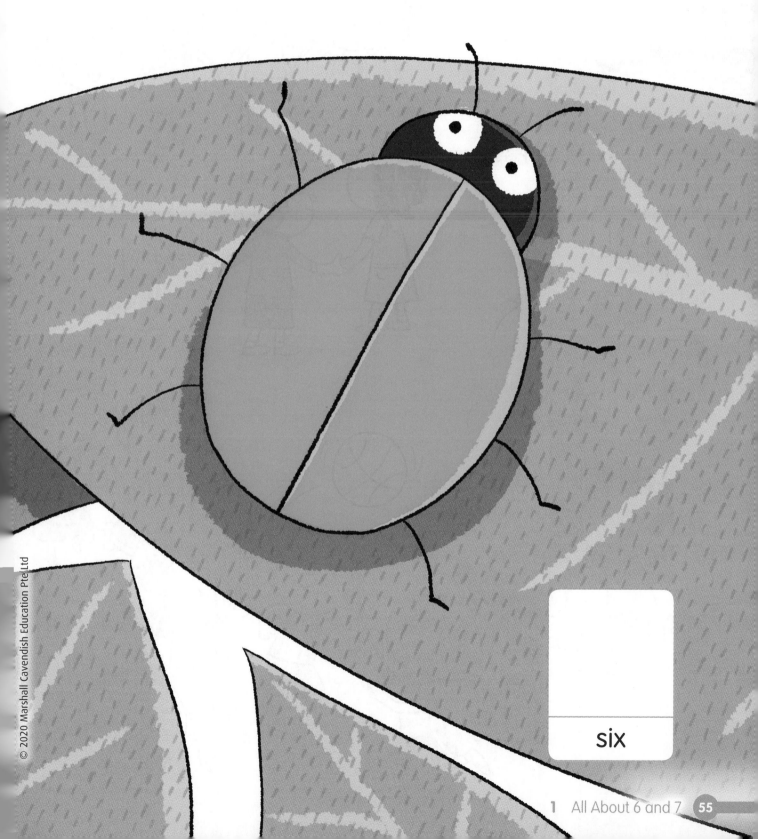

six

© 2020 Marshall Cavendish Education Pte Ltd

© 2020 Marshall Cavendish Education Pte Ltd

TRY

Match.

 1

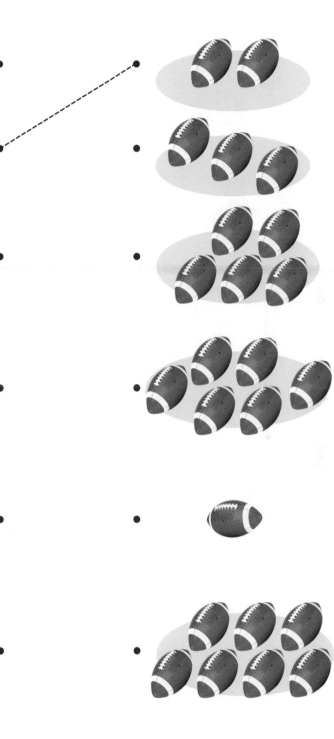

© 2020 Marshall Cavendish Education Pte Ltd

Count.
Color to show how many.

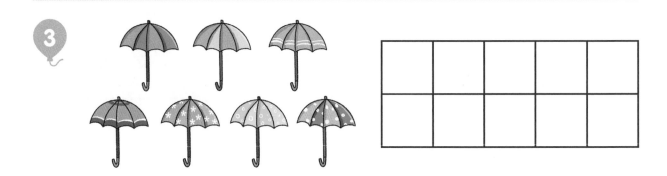

Trace each number.

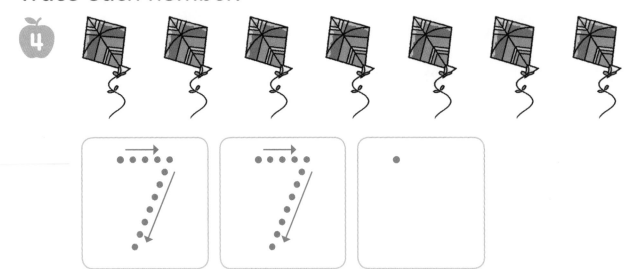

© 2020 Marshall Cavendish Education Pte Ltd

Count.
Write each number.

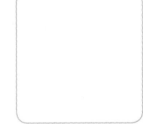

© 2020 Marshall Cavendish Education Pte Ltd

Draw 7 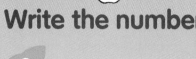.
Write the number.

8

seven

© 2020 Marshall Cavendish Education Pte Ltd

PRACTICE

Circle the groups of 6 in red.
Circle the groups of 7 in blue.

© 2020 Marshall Cavendish Education Pte Ltd

Count.
Write each number.

© 2020 Marshall Cavendish Education Pte Ltd

Draw the eggs.
Write each number.

 3 Draw six eggs.

six

4 Draw seven eggs.

seven

© 2020 Marshall Cavendish Education Pte Ltd

Count and match.

•   •

•   •

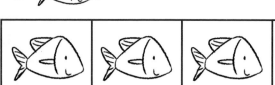 six   seven

Color 6 .

Draw 7 ◯.

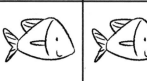

© 2020 Marshall Cavendish Education Pte Ltd

2 All About 8 and 9

LEARN All about number 8

© 2020 Marshall Cavendish Education Pte Ltd

Count.
Use  to show how you count.

© 2020 Marshall Cavendish Education Pte Ltd

Color to show each number.

5

6

7

8

© 2020 Marshall Cavendish Education Pte Ltd

Count.
Color to show how many.

 6

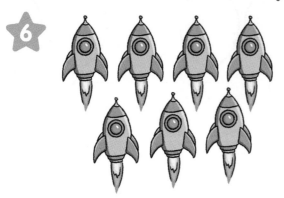

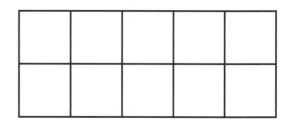

 **7**

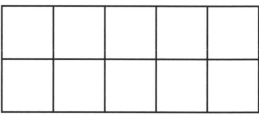

Trace each number.

 **8**

 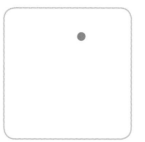

© 2020 Marshall Cavendish Education Pte Ltd

Count.
Write each number.

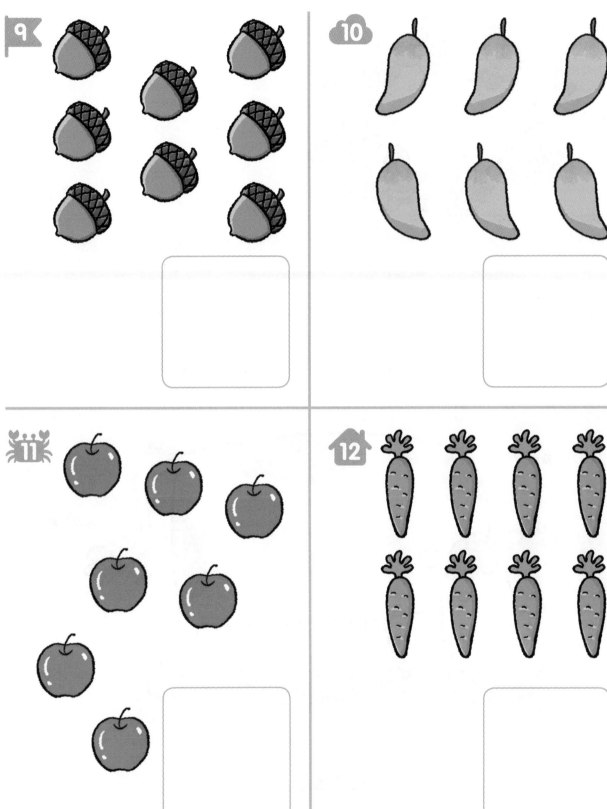

© 2020 Marshall Cavendish Education Pte Ltd

Count.
Write the number.

13

eight

Use 👆 to print eight spots on the 🐄.

Write the number.

14

eight

© 2020 Marshall Cavendish Education Pte Ltd

LEARN All about number 9

© 2020 Marshall Cavendish Education Pte Ltd

TRY

Match.

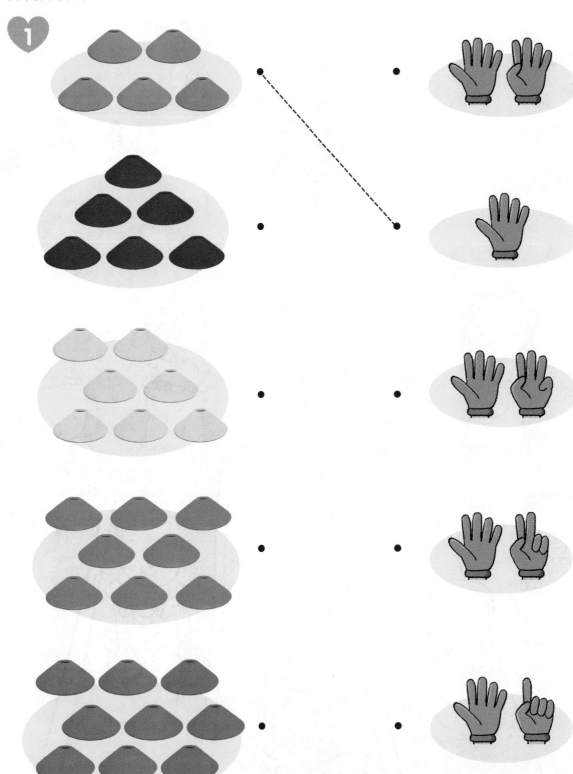

© 2020 Marshall Cavendish Education Pte Ltd

Count.
Use 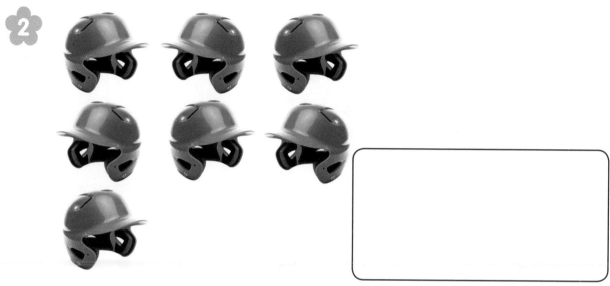 to show how you count.

2

3

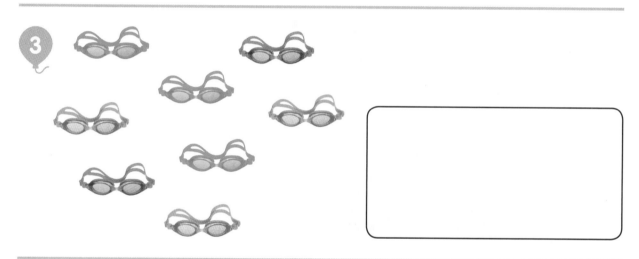

4

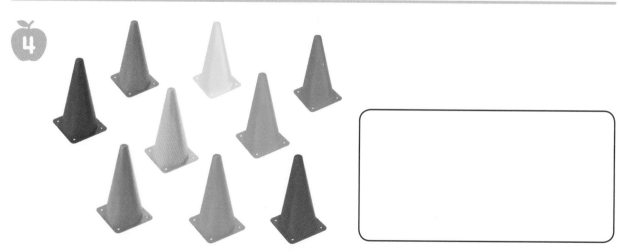

© 2020 Marshall Cavendish Education Pte Ltd

Count.
Color to show how many.

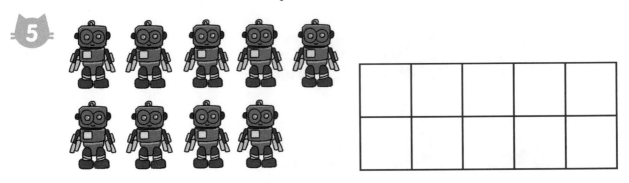

5

Trace each number.

6

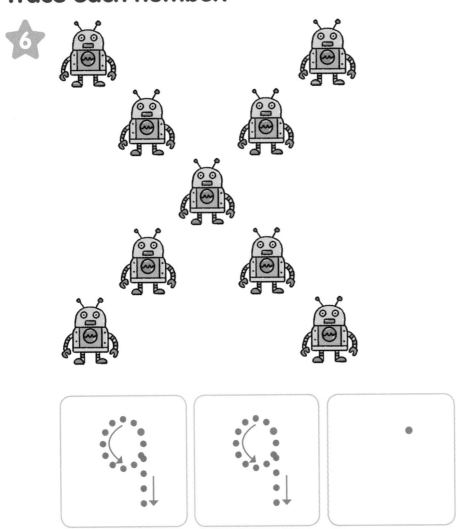

© 2020 Marshall Cavendish Education Pte Ltd

Count.
Write each number.

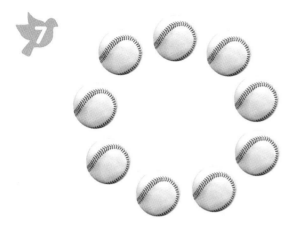

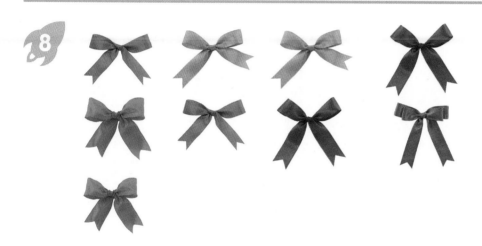

nine

© 2020 Marshall Cavendish Education Pte Ltd

Count.
Write each number.

10 Circle the group that has eight ⭐.

11 Circle the group that has nine ♡.

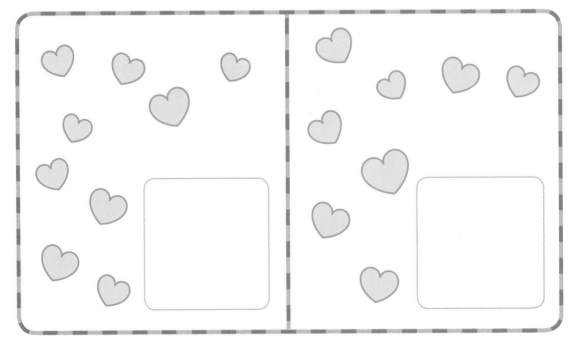

© 2020 Marshall Cavendish Education Pte Ltd

PRACTICE

Cut out the pictures below.
Glue the correct number of fruit in each bottle.

1 8 9

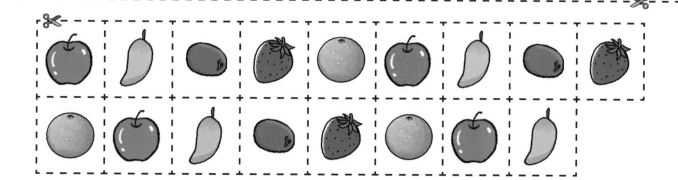

© 2020 Marshall Cavendish Education Pte Ltd

Count.
Write each number.

2

© 2020 Marshall Cavendish Education Pte Ltd

Draw the spots.
Write each number.

 3 Draw 8 spots.

eight

 4 Draw 9 spots.

nine

© 2020 Marshall Cavendish Education Pte Ltd

Count and match.

5

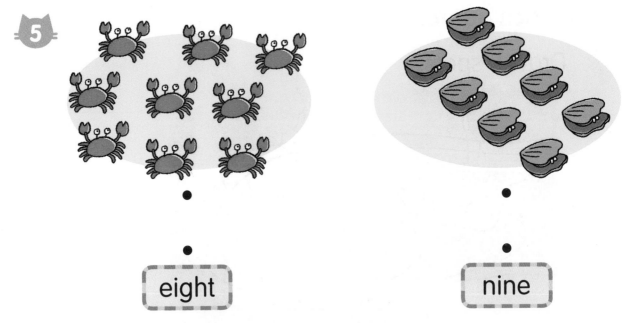

•

•

eight

•

•

nine

Color 8 🍎.

6

Draw 9 ◯.

7

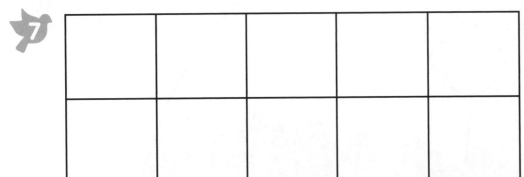

© 2020 Marshall Cavendish Education Pte Ltd

© 2020 Marshall Cavendish Education Pte Ltd

Name: _____ Date: _____

3 All About 10

LEARN All about number 10

TRY

Color the .

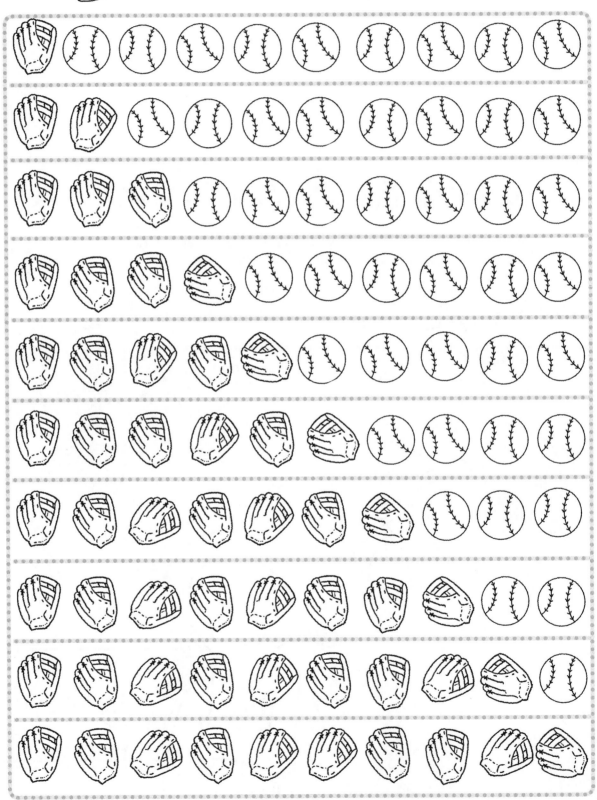

Count.
Use to show how you count.

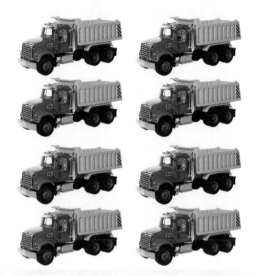 **2**

 3

 4

© 2020 Marshall Cavendish Education Pte Ltd

Trace each number.

 5

 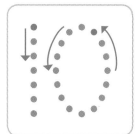 

Count.
Write each number.

 6

 7

© 2020 Marshall Cavendish Education Pte Ltd

Count and match.

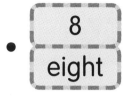

·   · 8
                        eight

·   · 9
                        nine

·   · 10
                        ten

© 2020 Marshall Cavendish Education Pte Ltd

Draw 10 raindrops.

ten

© 2020 Marshall Cavendish Education Pte Ltd

PRACTICE

Circle the groups of 10.

1

© 2020 Marshall Cavendish Education Pte Ltd

Trace each number.

Draw ten ⬭.

© 2020 Marshall Cavendish Education Pte Ltd

4 Order Numbers to 10

LEARN Order

© 2020 Marshall Cavendish Education Pte Ltd

TRY

Write each missing number.

1

6   7   8

2

4   5   7

3

10   9   8

4

5   6   9

© 2020 Marshall Cavendish Education Pte Ltd

PRACTICE

Write each missing number.

1. 2 3 4 5 ▢

2. 3 4 5 6 ▢

3. 9 ▢ 7 6 5

4. ▢ ▢ 8 7 6

© 2020 Marshall Cavendish Education Pte Ltd

Connect the dots in order.

© 2020 Marshall Cavendish Education Pte Ltd

© 2020 Marshall Cavendish Education Pte Ltd

Name: _____   Date: _____

5 Make Number Pairs to 10

LEARN Make number pairs of 2, 3, 4, and 5

TRY

Make number pairs.
Fill in each blank.

 1

1 and 1 make _____.

 2

1 and 2 make _____.

 3

2 and 1 make _____.

 4

 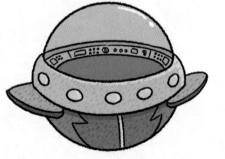

2 and 0 make _____.

94 Chapter 2 Numbers to 10

© 2020 Marshall Cavendish Education Pte Ltd

What numbers make 3?
Use red and blue to color.
Write each number.

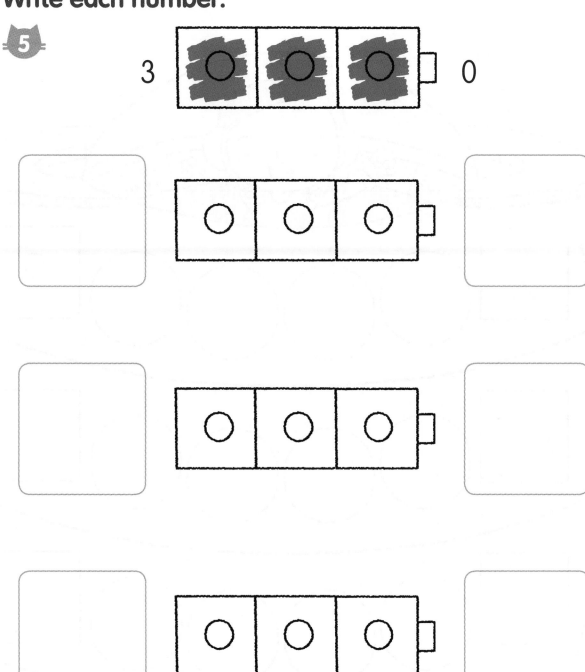

3   0

© 2020 Marshall Cavendish Education Pte Ltd

What numbers make 4?
Use  and ● to show.
Fill in each blank.

⭐ 6

What makes 4?

© 2020 Marshall Cavendish Education Pte Ltd

What numbers make 5?
Use ⬤ and ⬤ to show.
Fill in each blank.

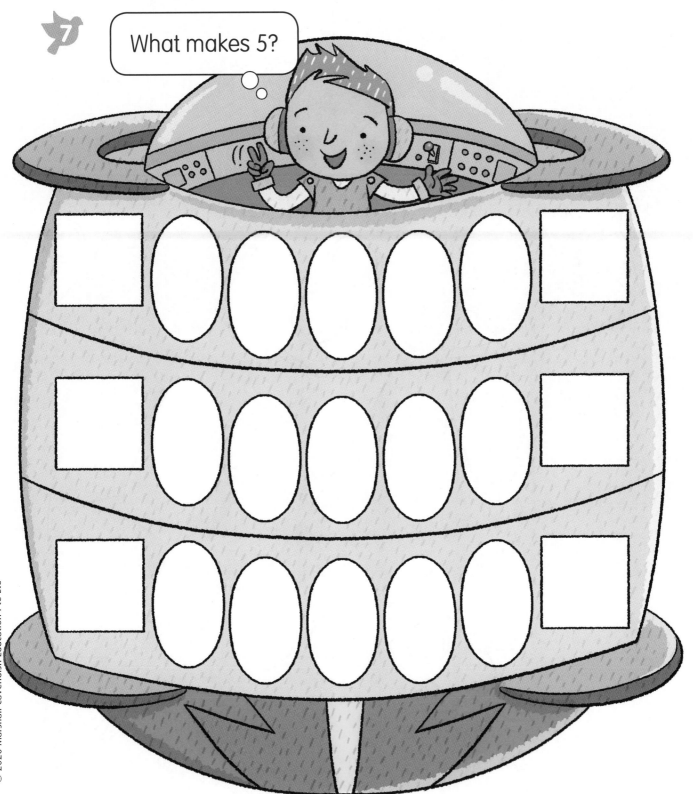

What makes 5?

© 2020 Marshall Cavendish Education Pte Ltd

© 2020 Marshall Cavendish Education Pte Ltd

TRY

What numbers make 6?
Use blue and orange to color.
Fill in each blank.

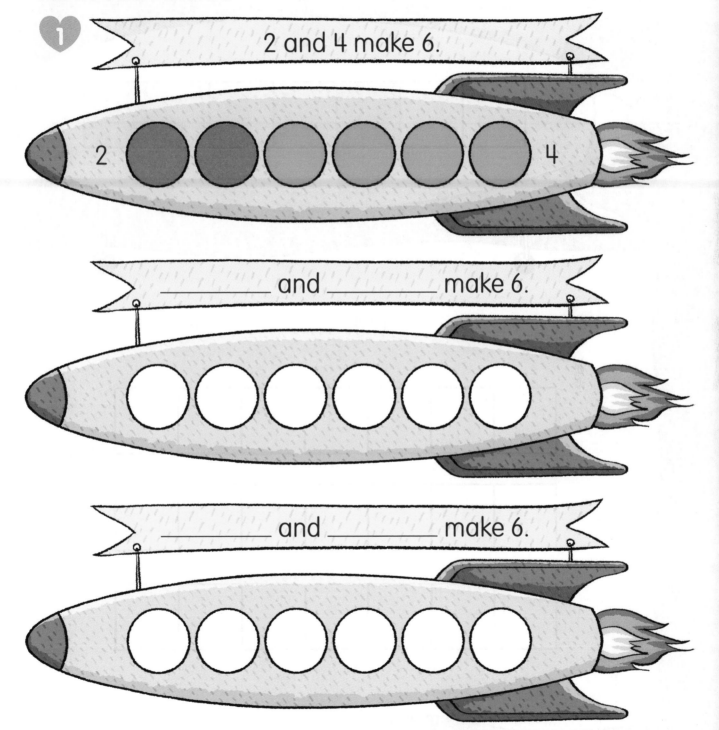

1 2 and 4 make 6.

2   4

_____ and _____ make 6.

_____ and _____ make 6.

© 2020 Marshall Cavendish Education Pte Ltd

What numbers make 7?
Use yellow and red to color.

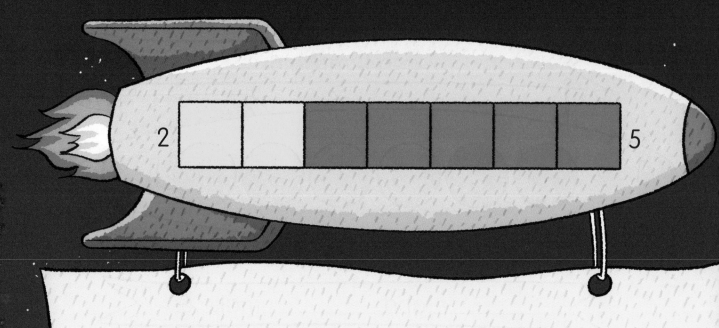

2 | | | | | | | 5

_____ and _____ make 7.

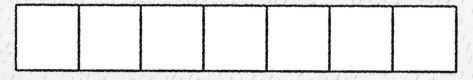

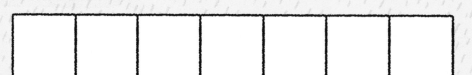

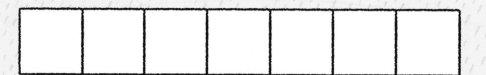

© 2020 Marshall Cavendish Education Pte Ltd

© 2020 Marshall Cavendish Education Pte Ltd

What numbers make 8?
Use blue and red to color.
Fill in each blank.

_____ and _____ make 8.

_____ and _____ make 8.

© 2020 Marshall Cavendish Education Pte Ltd

What numbers make 9?
Use ▪●▲ to decorate the robot.
Fill in each blank.

3

_____ and _____ make 9.

9 is _____ and _____.

© 2020 Marshall Cavendish Education Pte Ltd

LEARN Make number pairs of 10

© 2020 Marshall Cavendish Education Pte Ltd

What numbers make 10?
Use ◼●▲ to decorate the suit.
Fill in each blank.

♥ 1

What makes 10?

_____ and _____ make 10.

© 2020 Marshall Cavendish Education Pte Ltd

Find a new number pair for 10.
Use  **to decorate the suit.**
Fill in each blank.

2

_____ and _____ make _____.

_____ is _____ and _____.

© 2020 Marshall Cavendish Education Pte Ltd

PRACTICE

Fill in each blank.

5 and 2 make _____.

1 and _____ make _____.

_____ and _____ make 6.

© 2020 Marshall Cavendish Education Pte Ltd

Fill in each blank.
Draw dots to show each number pair.

 1 and 2 make _____.

---

 3 and _____ make 4.

 _____ and _____ make 5.

5 is _____ and _____.

© 2020 Marshall Cavendish Education Pte Ltd

6 Ordinal Numbers

LEARN Use ordinals to tell order

1st first
2nd second
3rd third
4th fourth
5th fifth
6th sixth
7th seventh
8th eighth
9th ninth
10th tenth

© 2020 Marshall Cavendish Education Pte Ltd

TRY

Circle.

 the 3rd button

1st

 the 5th chair

1st

Match.

| 7th | 1st | 4th | 2nd |

© 2020 Marshall Cavendish Education Pte Ltd

Three children had a race.
Number the pictures in the correct order.
Write 2nd, 3rd, or 4th.

© 2020 Marshall Cavendish Education Pte Ltd

SPIN THE WHEEL

What you need:

Players: 2

Materials: 40  for each player, , game board

What to do:

1 Player 1 spins the and stacks the correct number of on the game board.

2 Player 2 repeats 1 .

3 A player misses a turn if he or she spins a number that has been stacked.

4 Both players continue playing until all the numbers on the game board have been played.

Who is the winner?

The player to complete stacking for all the numbers first wins.

© 2020 Marshall Cavendish Education Pte Ltd

PRACTICE

© 2020 Marshall Cavendish Education Pte Ltd

Color the 2nd fish.

1st

Color the 4th apple.

1st

Color the 1st car orange.
Color the 3rd car red.

1st

Color the 1st bean red.
Color the 5th bean green.

4th

FINISH

Fill in each blank.
Write 2nd, 3rd, 4th, or 5th.

5

1st

Name: _____ Date: _____

 Count.
Write each number.

© 2020 Marshall Cavendish Education Pte Ltd

2 Alex, Ryan, and Jon are waiting in line.
Ryan is first.
Jon is not last.
Match each name to the correct boy.

Alex   Ryan   Jon

---

3 Use 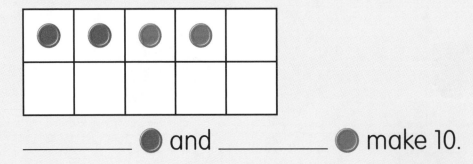 and ● to make 10.
Fill in each blank.

●	●	●	●	

_____ ● and _____ ● make 10.

© 2020 Marshall Cavendish Education Pte Ltd

MY MATH DICTIONARY

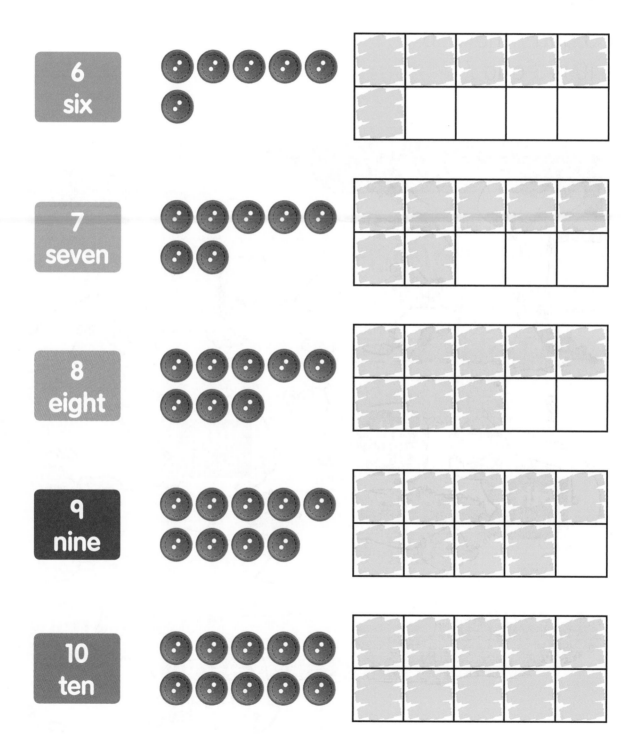

© 2020 Marshall Cavendish Education Pte Ltd

Number pairs

3 and 7 make 10.
10 is 3 and 7.

Ordinal numbers

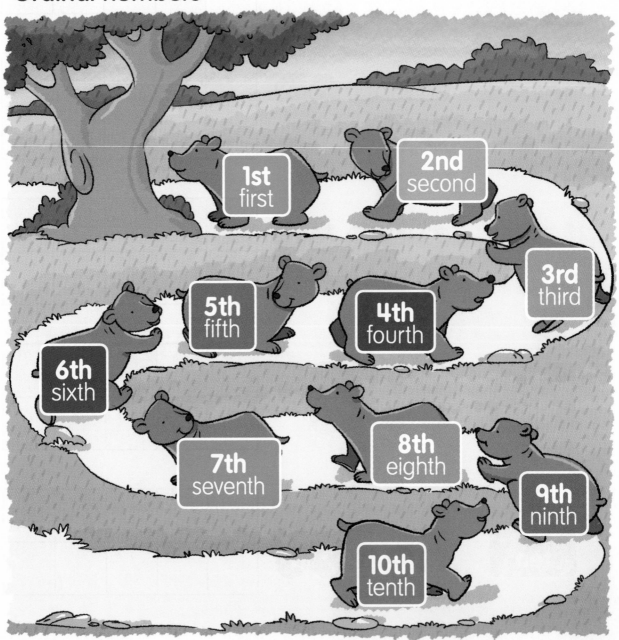

© 2020 Marshall Cavendish Education Pte Ltd

Name: _____ Date: _____

Count.
Write each number.

© 2020 Marshall Cavendish Education Pte Ltd

5

Write each missing number.

 6

7

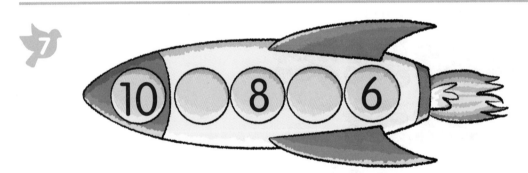

Fill in each blank.

 8

_____ and _____ make 5.

© 2020 Marshall Cavendish Education Pte Ltd

Look at the picture.
Circle the correct answer.

9 How many people are there?

7   8   9

10 Who is 1st?

11 Who is 4th?

© 2020 Marshall Cavendish Education Pte Ltd

Assessment Prep
Answer each question.

 12 Circle the group that shows 6.

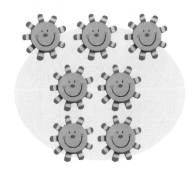 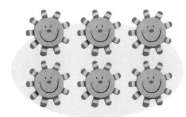

---

 13 Circle the groups that show 9.

---

 14 Color all the boxes with the correct sentences.

| 5 and 2 make 7. | 7 is 2 and 6. |
| 2 and 5 make 7. | 7 is 2 and 5. |

© 2020 Marshall Cavendish Education Pte Ltd

Name: _____ Date: _____

Put on a Show

 1 Chris hangs some stars on a wall.

a Color to show how many there are.

b How many stars are there?
Write the number.

c Color the correct box to complete the sentence.

Chris hangs  stars.

© 2020 Marshall Cavendish Education Pte Ltd

2 Laila draws some butterflies on the wall.

1st

a Color the 1st butterfly **blue**.

b Color the 3rd butterfly **green**.

c Color the 5th butterfly **red**.

d How many butterflies does Laila draw?
Write the number.

e Draw another butterfly.
Use ⬤ to show how many there are.

© 2020 Marshall Cavendish Education Pte Ltd

© 2020 Marshall Cavendish Education Pte Ltd

1 Compare Lengths

LEARN Compare the lengths of two objects

© 2020 Marshall Cavendish Education Pte Ltd

Draw a long tail.

Draw a short tail.

© 2020 Marshall Cavendish Education Pte Ltd

Circle the longer object.
Make an X on the shorter object.

3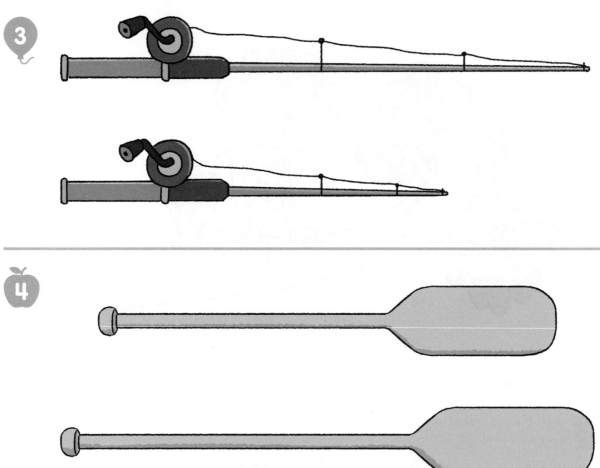

4

5

© 2020 Marshall Cavendish Education Pte Ltd

Color the shorter object in each pair.
Circle the longer object in each pair.

⭐ 6

© 2020 Marshall Cavendish Education Pte Ltd

Which have the same length?
Circle them.

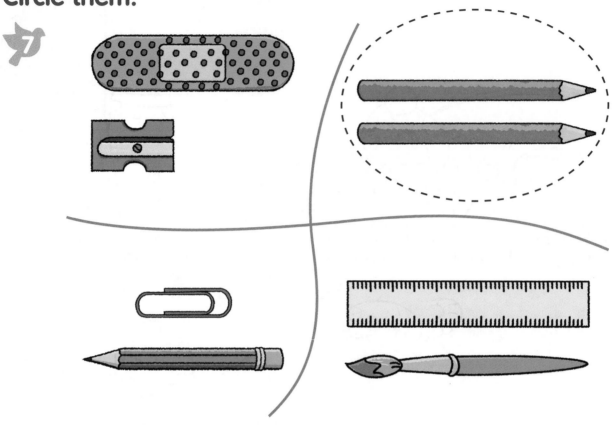

Look at the pictures above.
Color each box with the correct sentence.

8 The 🩹 is as long as the ✏️.

9 The ✏️ is as long as the ✏️.

10 The 📏 is as long as the 🖌️.

© 2020 Marshall Cavendish Education Pte Ltd

Circle the shorter .

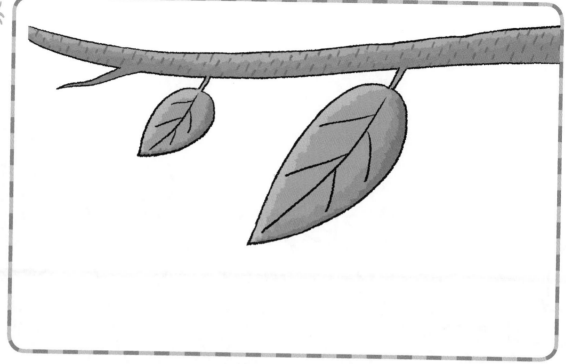

Draw a line that is longer than the .

© 2020 Marshall Cavendish Education Pte Ltd

LEARN Measure length

© 2020 Marshall Cavendish Education Pte Ltd

TRY

Find the length of each picture.
Use .
Fill in each blank.

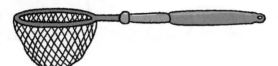

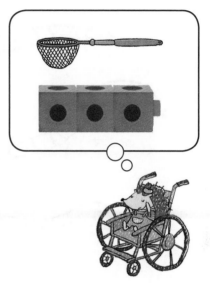

The is about _____ long.

2

The  is about _____ long.

3

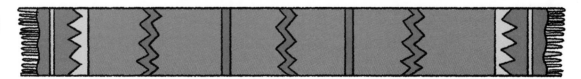

The is about _____ long.

© 2020 Marshall Cavendish Education Pte Ltd

Find the length of each snake.
Use .
Fill in each blank.

4  is about ________  long.

5  is about ________  long.

6  is about ________  long.

7  is about ________  long.

© 2020 Marshall Cavendish Education Pte Ltd

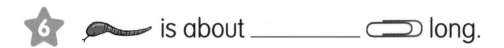

Count the ⬭.
Fill in each blank.

⬭⬭ ⬭⬭

1   2

The 📅 is about _____ ⬭ long.

⬭ ⬭ ⬭ ⬭ ⬭

The ☂ is about _____ ⬭ long.

Which is longer?

📅 or ☂ ?

Which is shorter?

© 2020 Marshall Cavendish Education Pte Ltd

Look for these objects.
Use **and** **to find the lengths.**
Fill in each blank.

10

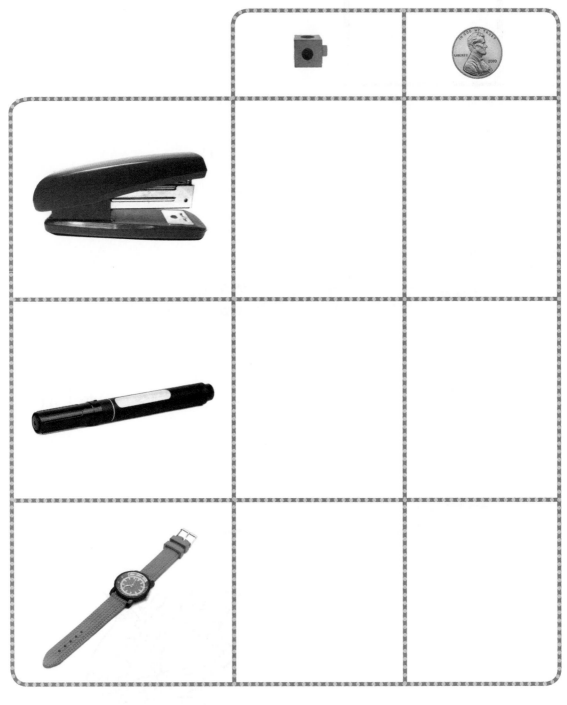

© 2020 Marshall Cavendish Education Pte Ltd

Name: _____   Date: _____

PRACTICE

Draw a short tail.

Draw a long tail.

© 2020 Marshall Cavendish Education Pte Ltd

Which is longer?
Color it.
Which is shorter?
Make an X on it.

3

4

5

© 2020 Marshall Cavendish Education Pte Ltd

Color the 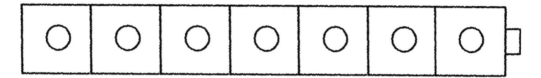 to show the lengths.

 6

 7

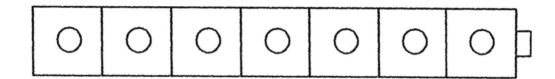

 **8**

© 2020 Marshall Cavendish Education Pte Ltd

Count the _____.
Fill in each blank.

© 2020 Marshall Cavendish Education Pte Ltd

9

_____ _____ _____

The is about _____ _____ long.

10

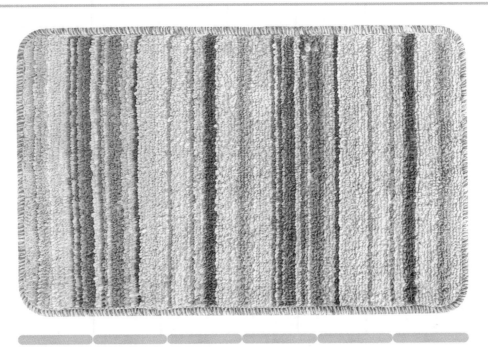

_____ _____ _____ _____ _____ _____

The ▥ is about _____ _____ long.

2 Compare Heights

LEARN Compare the heights of two objects

© 2020 Marshall Cavendish Education Pte Ltd

Draw a tall candle.

Draw a short candle.

© 2020 Marshall Cavendish Education Pte Ltd

Which is taller?
Circle it.
Which is shorter?
Make an X on it.

 3

 4

© 2020 Marshall Cavendish Education Pte Ltd

Make an X on the shorter object.
If they have the same height, circle them both.

© 2020 Marshall Cavendish Education Pte Ltd

Look at the trees.
Color the correct box to complete each sentence.

a   The 🌲 is

shorter than
taller than

the 🌱 .

b   The 🌱 is

shorter than
taller than

the 🌲 .

© 2020 Marshall Cavendish Education Pte Ltd

Circle the animal that is taller than the .

 12

Circle the object that is shorter than the .

 13

© 2020 Marshall Cavendish Education Pte Ltd

TRY

Find the height of each picture.
Use .
Fill in each blank.

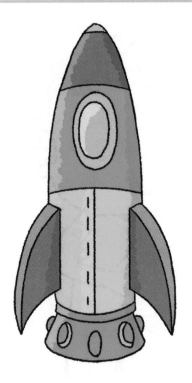

The is about _____ tall.

2

The is about _____ tall.

© 2020 Marshall Cavendish Education Pte Ltd

Count the .
Fill in each blank.

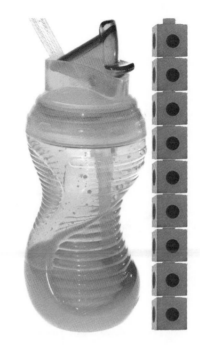

3 The  is about _____  tall.

4 The  is about _____  tall.

5 The  is about _____  tall.

Which is shorter?

 or ?

Which is taller?

 or ?

© 2020 Marshall Cavendish Education Pte Ltd

Look for these objects.
Use 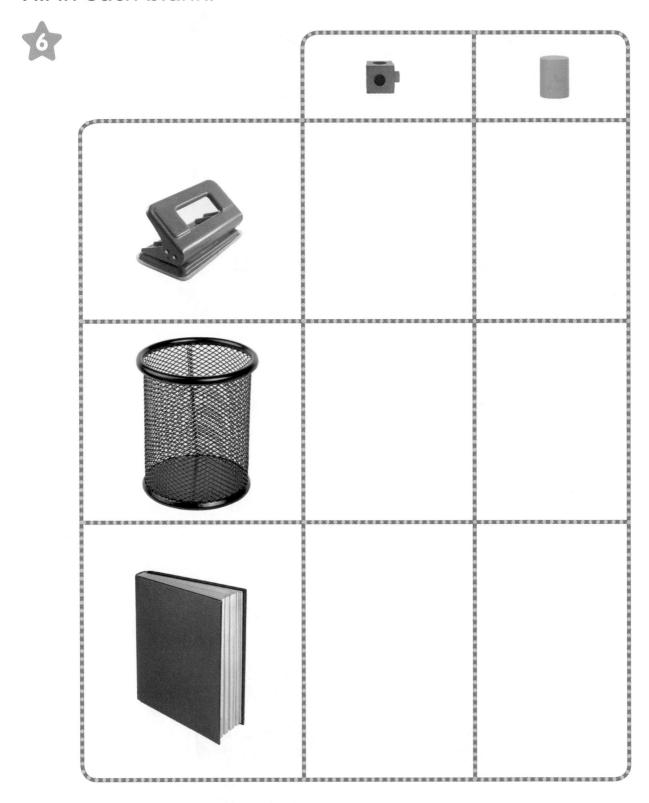 and ▯ to find each height.
Fill in each blank.

★6

© 2020 Marshall Cavendish Education Pte Ltd

Name: _____ Date: _____

PRACTICE

Which animal is taller?
Color it.
Which animal is shorter?
Circle it.

© 2020 Marshall Cavendish Education Pte Ltd

Circle the object that is taller than the .

 4

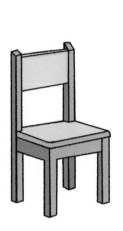

Color the object that is as tall as Lucas.

 5

Lucas

© 2020 Marshall Cavendish Education Pte Ltd

Look for these objects.
Use  to find each height.
Fill in each blank.

A mug is about _____ tall.

A water bottle is about _____ tall.

Use  to find the heights.
How are your answers different from ⭐6 and 🕊7 ?

© 2020 Marshall Cavendish Education Pte Ltd

Count the  **.**
Fill in each blank.

8

The 🪣 is about _____ 🟢🟣 tall.

9

The 🏺 is about _____ 🟡🟣 tall.

10

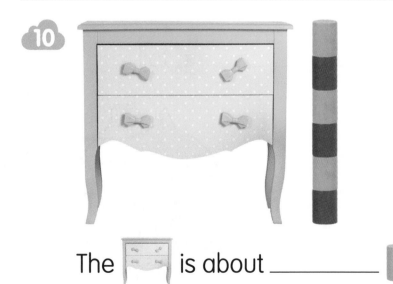

The 🗄 is about _____ 🟡🟣 tall.

© 2020 Marshall Cavendish Education Pte Ltd

© 2020 Marshall Cavendish Education Pte Ltd

Name: _____ Date: _____

3 Compare Lengths, Heights, and Weights

LEARN Compare the weights of two objects

TRY

Which fruit is heavy?
Circle.

 1

© 2020 Marshall Cavendish Education Pte Ltd

Which is heavier?
Make an X on it.
Which is lighter?
Circle it.

 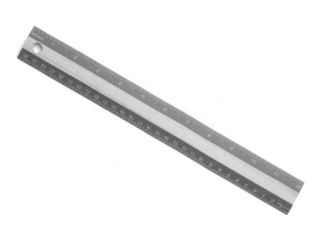

© 2020 Marshall Cavendish Education Pte Ltd

Make an X on the heavier object.
If they have the same weight, circle them both.

 5

 6

 7

© 2020 Marshall Cavendish Education Pte Ltd

LEARN Compare lengths, heights, and weights

© 2020 Marshall Cavendish Education Pte Ltd

TRY

Which is taller?
Circle it.
Which is heavier?
Make an X on it.

© 2020 Marshall Cavendish Education Pte Ltd

1

2

3

Find two objects that are longer and heavier than a .

Draw or glue a picture below.

© 2020 Marshall Cavendish Education Pte Ltd

Color the correct box to complete each sentence.

a   The 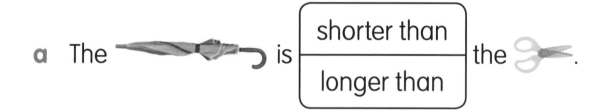 is

shorter than
longer than

the ✂.

b   The ✂ is

lighter than
heavier than

the ☂.

© 2020 Marshall Cavendish Education Pte Ltd

Color the correct box to complete each sentence.

a The is

lighter than
heavier than

the .

b The is

shorter than
taller than

the .

© 2020 Marshall Cavendish Education Pte Ltd

LENGTH RACE!

What you need:

Players: 2

Materials: 1 set of for each player

What to do:

1 Shuffle your .

2 Count to three. Then put your in a line.

Who is the winner?

The first player to line up all of his or her correctly wins.

© 2020 Marshall Cavendish Education Pte Ltd

PRACTICE

Which objects are light?
Circle them.

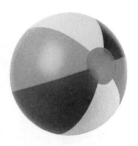

© 2020 Marshall Cavendish Education Pte Ltd

Which is heavier?
Circle it.
Which is lighter?
Make an X on it.

 2

 3

 4

© 2020 Marshall Cavendish Education Pte Ltd

Which can you lift by yourself?
Circle them.

© 2020 Marshall Cavendish Education Pte Ltd

Which ball is as heavy as ?

Draw two objects that have the same weight.

© 2020 Marshall Cavendish Education Pte Ltd

Which is longer?
Circle it.
Which is lighter?
Make an X on it.

 8

9

10

© 2020 Marshall Cavendish Education Pte Ltd

Find two objects that are taller and lighter than a .

Collect pictures and glue them below.

© 2020 Marshall Cavendish Education Pte Ltd

Name: _____ Date: _____

 1 Find the length of each strip of paper.

    a Use

    The strip of paper is about _____ ⌒ long.

    b Use ▬▬▬

    The strip of paper is about _____
    ▬▬▬ long.

    c Choose another object other than ⌒ and ▬▬▬.
    Use it to measure this strip of paper.

    The strip of paper is about _____ long.

© 2020 Marshall Cavendish Education Pte Ltd

2

a What is longer and lighter than your math book? Draw or glue a picture below.

b What is shorter and heavier than your math book? Draw or glue a picture below.

© 2020 Marshall Cavendish Education Pte Ltd

MY MATH DICTIONARY

Length

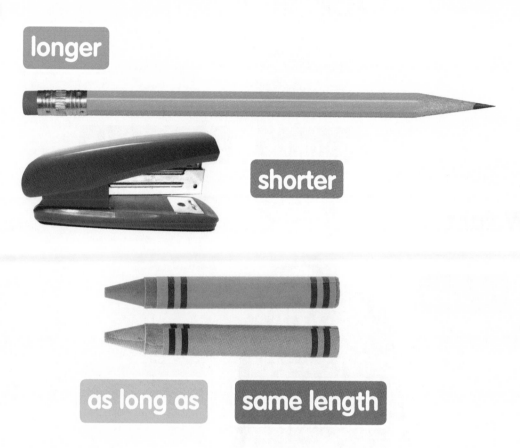

longer

shorter

as long as   same length

Height

taller

GLUE

shorter

© 2020 Marshall Cavendish Education Pte Ltd

as tall as   same height

Weight

heavier

lighter

as heavy as

same weight

© 2020 Marshall Cavendish Education Pte Ltd

Name: _____ Date: _____

Draw a short tail.
Draw a tall hat.

Which is longer?
Circle it.
Which is shorter?
Make an X on it.

© 2020 Marshall Cavendish Education Pte Ltd

Find the length of the .
Use .
Fill in the blank.

The is about _____ long.

Count the ▬▬▬.
Fill in each blank.

5

The ⬤⬤⬤ is about _____ ▬▬▬ long.

6

The ▭ is about _____ ▬▬▬ long.

© 2020 Marshall Cavendish Education Pte Ltd

Color the heavier object blue.
Color the lighter object green.

Color the taller object blue.
Color the shorter object green.

 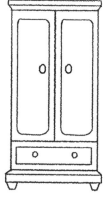

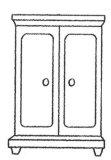

© 2020 Marshall Cavendish Education Pte Ltd

Find the height of the picture.
Use .
Fill in the blank.

10

The MILK is about _____ tall.

Count the .
Fill in the blank.

11

The 🥤 is about _____ tall.

© 2020 Marshall Cavendish Education Pte Ltd

Assessment Prep
Answer each question.

© 2020 Marshall Cavendish Education Pte Ltd

12 Which are too heavy to lift by yourself?
Circle them.
Which are taller than you?
Make an ✗ on them.

Color the correct box to complete each sentence.

a   The is

shorter than
taller than

the .

b   The 🫙 is

shorter than
taller than

the .

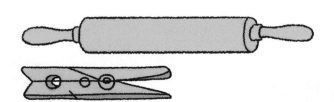

a   The 🥖 is

heavier than
lighter than

the 📎.

b   The 📎 is

longer than
shorter than

the 🥖.

© 2020 Marshall Cavendish Education Pte Ltd

Name: _____ Date: _____

Camping Trip

 1 Look at the pictures below.
Which are longer than your arm?
Circle them.

© 2020 Marshall Cavendish Education Pte Ltd

2 Find the length of your table.

Use your .

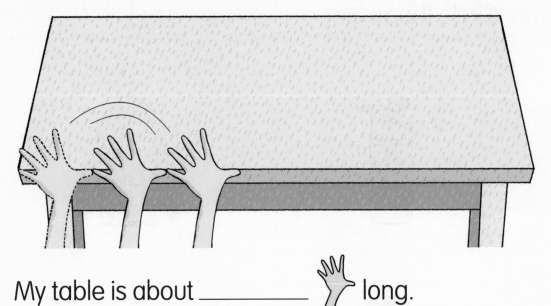

My table is about _____ 🖐 long.

---

3 What is shorter than your 🖐?
Draw or glue a picture below.

© 2020 Marshall Cavendish Education Pte Ltd

© 2020 Marshall Cavendish Education Pte Ltd

1 More Than

LEARN Compare using **more than**

© 2020 Marshall Cavendish Education Pte Ltd

Match each to a .

Circle the group that has **more**.

 1

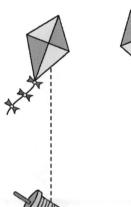

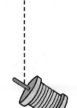

Match each to a .

Circle the group that has **more**.

 2

© 2020 Marshall Cavendish Education Pte Ltd

Match and compare.
Color each correct box.

 3

There are **more** than .

There are **more** than  .

 4

There are **more** than .

There are **more** than .

© 2020 Marshall Cavendish Education Pte Ltd

There are **more** than 🧱.

There are **more** 🧱 than .

© 2020 Marshall Cavendish Education Pte Ltd

Answer each question.

a Draw ◯ to show more .

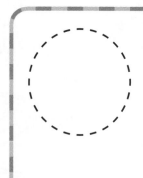

b How many ◯ did you draw?

© 2020 Marshall Cavendish Education Pte Ltd

PRACTICE

Match and compare.
Circle the group that has more.

 1

 2

© 2020 Marshall Cavendish Education Pte Ltd

Compare.
Circle the group that has more.

3

4

5

© 2020 Marshall Cavendish Education Pte Ltd

2 Fewer Than

LEARN Compare using fewer than

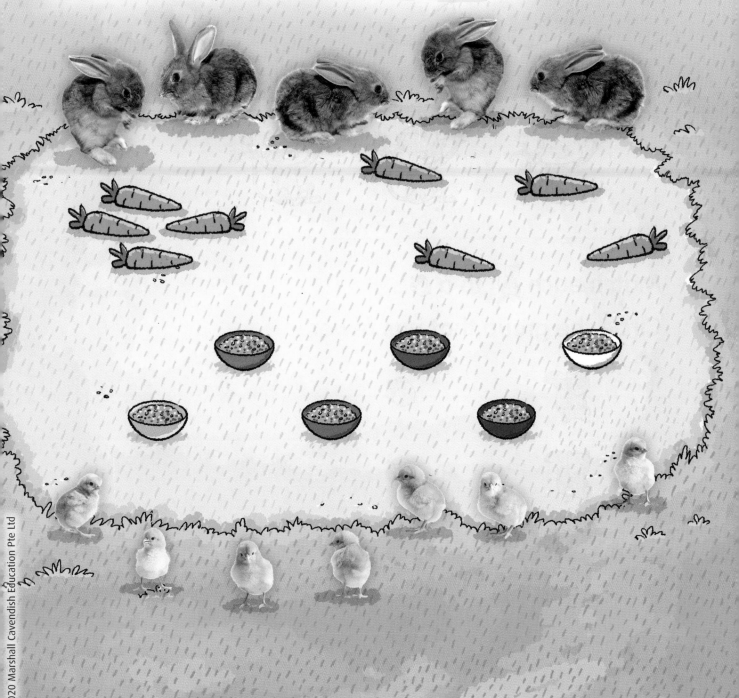

© 2020 Marshall Cavendish Education Pte Ltd

TRY

Match each  to a 🐵.

Circle the group that has **fewer**.

1

Match each to a 🌰.

Circle the group that has **fewer**.

2

© 2020 Marshall Cavendish Education Pte Ltd

Match and compare.
Color the correct box to complete each sentence.

There are
fewer
more
 than .

There are
more
fewer
 than .

© 2020 Marshall Cavendish Education Pte Ltd

Match and compare.
Color the correct box to complete each sentence.

5

There are [more / fewer] 🐟 than 🎣 .

There are [fewer / more] 🎣 than 🐟 .

© 2020 Marshall Cavendish Education Pte Ltd

Compare.
Color each correct box.

There are **fewer** 🌻 than 🌼 .

There are **fewer** 🌼 than 🌻 .

There are **fewer** 🐭 than 🍓 .

There are **fewer** 🍓 than 🐭 .

© 2020 Marshall Cavendish Education Pte Ltd

Answer each question.

a Draw 🎈 to show fewer 🎈.

b How many 🎈 did you draw?

© 2020 Marshall Cavendish Education Pte Ltd

Name: _____   Date: _____

PRACTICE

Compare.
Color the correct box.

There are **fewer** 🍎 than 🍐.

There are **fewer** 🍐 than 🍎.

© 2020 Marshall Cavendish Education Pte Ltd

Compare.
Circle the group that has fewer.

  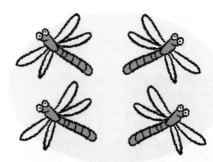

  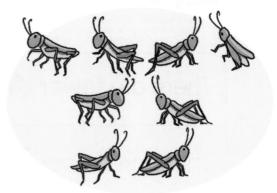

© 2020 Marshall Cavendish Education Pte Ltd

3 Same

LEARN Compare using the same

© 2020 Marshall Cavendish Education Pte Ltd

TRY

Match and compare.
Color each correct box.

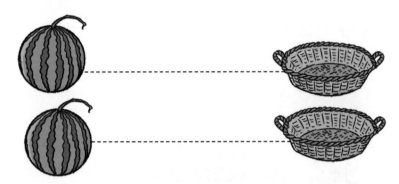

There are **more** than  .

The number of and is **the same**.

The number of and is **the same**.

There are **fewer** than .

© 2020 Marshall Cavendish Education Pte Ltd

The number of  and is **the same**.

There are **more** than .

There are **fewer** than .

There are **more** than .

© 2020 Marshall Cavendish Education Pte Ltd

Draw the same number of  as 🦢.

5

© 2020 Marshall Cavendish Education Pte Ltd

Name: _____   Date: _____

PRACTICE

Match and compare.
Color Yes or No.

 1

Is the number of   and the same?

Yes
No

 2

Is the number of and the same?

Yes
No

© 2020 Marshall Cavendish Education Pte Ltd

Compare.
Color Yes or No.

 3

Is the number of  and 🥚 the same?

Yes
No

Compare.
Circle all the groups with the same number.

 4

 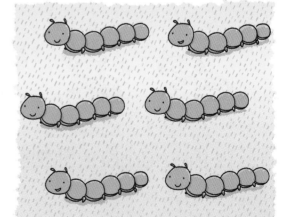

© 2020 Marshall Cavendish Education Pte Ltd

4 Compare Numbers to 10

LEARN Compare two numbers using greater than, less than, and the same

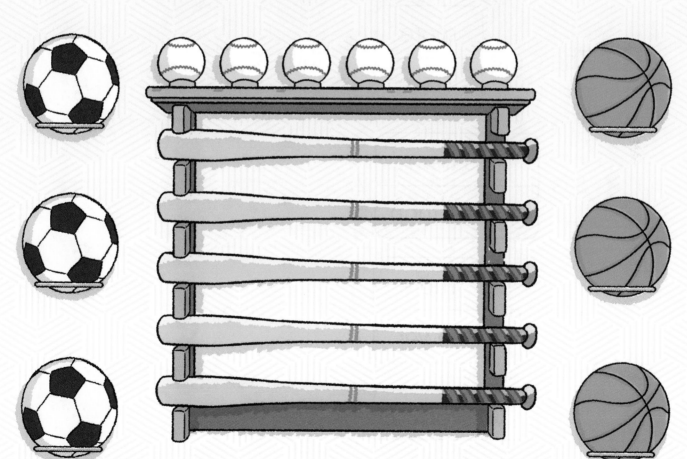

© 2020 Marshall Cavendish Education Pte Ltd

TRY

Write each number.
Compare.
Color the correct box to complete each sentence.

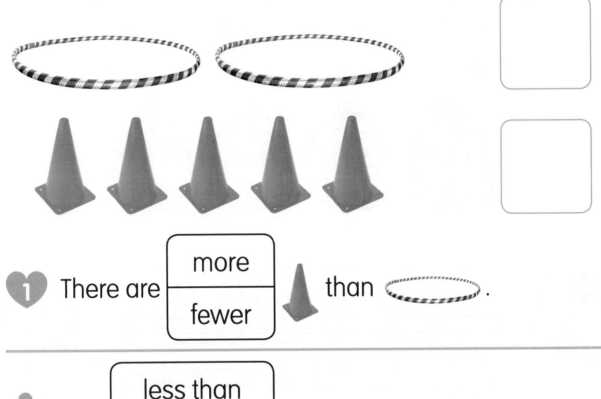

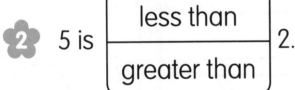

1 There are [more / fewer] 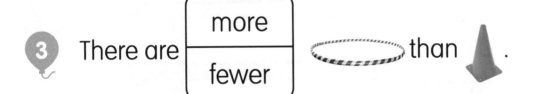 than ⬭ .

2 5 is [less than / greater than] 2.

3 There are [more / fewer] ⬭ than ▲ .

4 2 is [less than / greater than] 5.

© 2020 Marshall Cavendish Education Pte Ltd

Write each number.
Compare.
Color the correct box to complete each sentence.

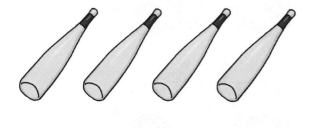

 5 The number of and is the same.

6 4 is

| less than |
| the same as |
| greater than |

4.

© 2020 Marshall Cavendish Education Pte Ltd

Color the circles with numbers greater than 5.

7

3   8

5   6

9   2

Compare and color.

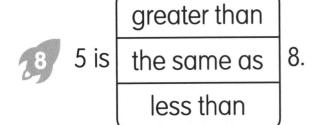

8

5 is
| greater than |
| the same as |
| less than |
8.

Fill in the blank.

9 _____ is greater than 3.

© 2020 Marshall Cavendish Education Pte Ltd

1 more

1 less

Write each number.
Color the correct box to complete each sentence.

3 is
1 more than
1 less than
4.

4 is
1 more than
1 less than
3.

Write each number.
Compare the numbers.

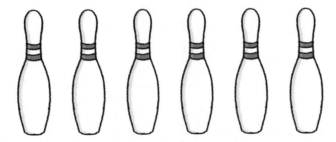

_____ 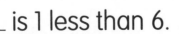 is 1 less than 6.

_____ is 1 more than 5.

© 2020 Marshall Cavendish Education Pte Ltd

Write each number.
Circle the group that shows 1 more.
Fill in each blank.

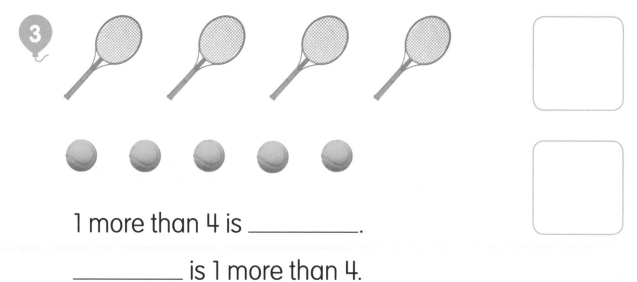

3

1 more than 4 is _____.

_____ is 1 more than 4.

Draw 🔍 to show 1 more.

4

How many are there now?

© 2020 Marshall Cavendish Education Pte ltd

Write each number.
Circle the group that shows 1 less.
Fill in each blank.

1 less than 7 is _____.

_____ is 1 less than 7.

Make an X to show 1 less.

How many are there now?

© 2020 Marshall Cavendish Education Pte Ltd

Read the story.

 Maya has 3 .

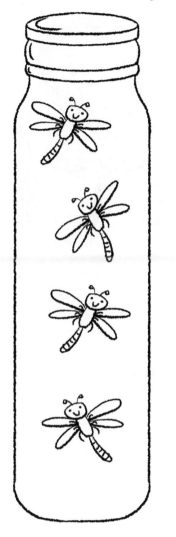

Color Maya's jar.
Make an ✗ on the jar that shows **1 more**.
Circle the jar that shows **1 less**.

© 2020 Marshall Cavendish Education Pte Ltd

TAP

What you need:

Players: 2

Materials: 1 set of , set of ,

What to do:

1. Shuffle the cards. Each player receives an equal number of cards.

2. Each player puts his or her cards face down.

3. Each player draws a card from his or her stack of cards. Turn it over and place it in the center. Compare the numbers. Use to help you. Tap the card with the greater number.

4. The player who taps the correct card first keeps both cards.

5. Keep playing until all the cards are gone.

Who is the winner?

The player with the most cards wins.

© 2020 Marshall Cavendish Education Pte Ltd

PRACTICE

Count and write each number.
Color the correct box to complete each sentence.

1

6 is	greater than	4.
	less than	

4 is	greater than	6.
	less than	

Circle the group(s) that has **more than 5**.
Make an **X** on the group(s) that has **fewer than 5**.

2

© 2020 Marshall Cavendish Education Pte Ltd

Read each story.

a Claire has 7 .
She has the same number of 👕 as 🧢.
How many 👕 does Claire have?
Draw 👕 to show the number.
Write the number.

b Claire has fewer ▮ than 👕.
How many ▮ do you think Claire has?
Write the number.

© 2020 Marshall Cavendish Education Pte Ltd

Circle the group that shows 1 more.

© 2020 Marshall Cavendish Education Pte Ltd

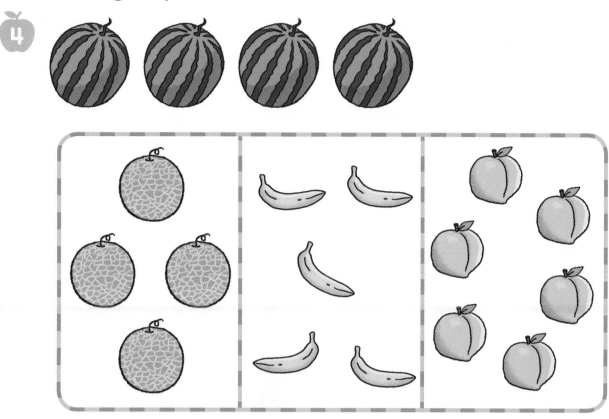

Circle the group that shows 1 less.

Count the prints.
Write the number.
Make 1 less and 1 more.
Write the numbers.

1 less than		1 more than
	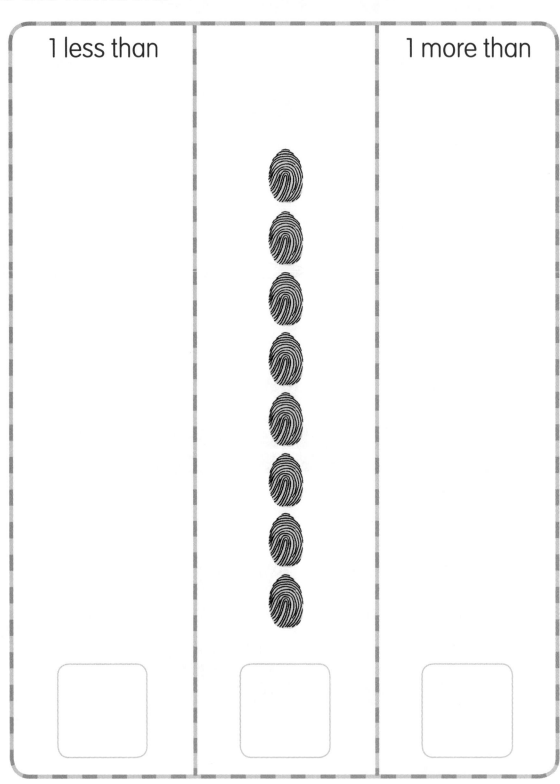	

© 2020 Marshall Cavendish Education Pte Ltd

Name: _____ Date: _____

1 **a** Count.
Circle the group that shows a greater number.

b Make both groups have the same number.
Draw to show your answer.

2 Circle numbers greater than 1.

| 0 | 1 | 2 | 3 | 4 | 5 |

3 Make an ✗ on numbers less than 4.

| 0 | 1 | 2 | 3 | 4 | 5 |

© 2020 Marshall Cavendish Education Pte Ltd

4 Sara writes two numbers.
The numbers are greater than 1.
They are less than 4.
What are they?
Draw 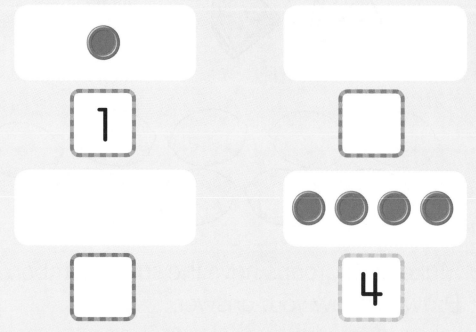 to show the numbers.

5 Write each missing number.

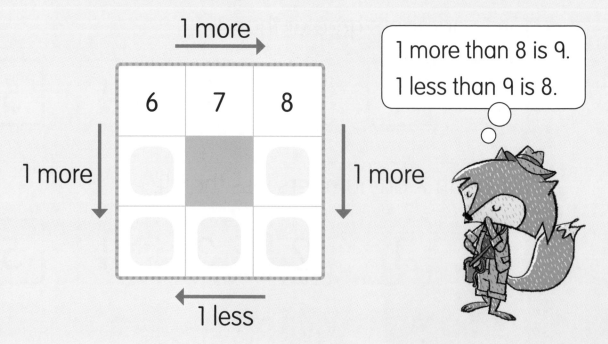

1 more than 8 is 9.
1 less than 9 is 8.

© 2020 Marshall Cavendish Education Pte Ltd

MY MATH DICTIONARY

more than

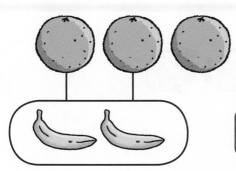

fewer than

the same

© 2020 Marshall Cavendish Education Pte Ltd

5 is **greater than** 4.
4 is **less than** 5.

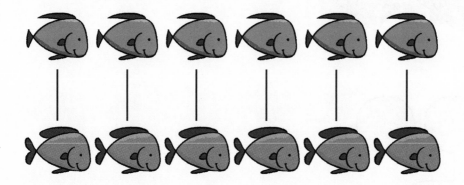

The number of red fish is **the same** as the number of blue fish.

1 more than 2 is 3.
3 is **1 more** than 2.

1 less than 3 is 2.
2 is **1 less** than 3

© 2020 Marshall Cavendish Education Pte Ltd

Name: _____ Date: _____

Circle the group with more.

Circle the group with fewer.

Circle the groups that have the same number of ●.

© 2020 Marshall Cavendish Education Pte Ltd

Match and compare.
Color the correct box to complete each sentence.

 4 There are
fewer
more
 than .

 5 There are
fewer
more
 than  .

 6 5 is
less than
greater than
7.

7 7 is
less than
greater than
5.

© 2020 Marshall Cavendish Education Pte Ltd

Answer each question.

 a Draw 5 🍎.

> (empty box)

b Naomi has some 🍊.
The number of 🍊 is **1 less than** the number of 🍎.
Draw the 🍊 that Naomi has.

> (empty box)

Write 1, 7, or 9.

 9 3 is greater than _____.

 10 7 is less than _____.

 11 1 more than _____ is 8.

© 2020 Marshall Cavendish Education Pte Ltd

Assessment Prep
Answer each question.

 12 Which sentences are correct?
Color the boxes.

6 is equal to 5.	1 less than 5 is 6.
1 more than 5 is 6.	6 is greater than 5.

---

13 Noah has 4 .

Kayla has 1 more than Noah.

John has 1 less than Noah.

Make an ✗ on the group that John has.

Circle the group of Kayla has.

© 2020 Marshall Cavendish Education Pte Ltd

Name: _____ Date: _____

By the River

 1 Joe is at the river.
He sees 3 fish.
He shows the number with his fingers.

a Hold up 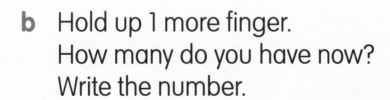 .
Hold up 1 more finger.
How many do you have now?
Write the number.

b Hold up 1 more finger.
How many do you have now?
Write the number.

c How many is 1 less than ✌?
Write the number.

© 2020 Marshall Cavendish Education Pte Ltd

Ella sees some  in a river.

How many does she see?
Write the number.

Kris sees more  than Ella.
Draw  to show more .

How many  does Kris see?
Write the number.

© 2020 Marshall Cavendish Education Pte Ltd

3 Lucy counts some  in a pond.

How many 🐢 does she count?
Write the number.

Luke counts some 🐢 in a pond too.
He counts 1 less 🐢 than Lucy.
Draw 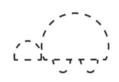 to show the 🐢 that Luke counts.

How many 🐢 does Luke count?
Write the number.

© 2020 Marshall Cavendish Education Pte Ltd

Mai puts some water in the .

How many does she use?
Write the number.

Adam uses the same number of .
Draw 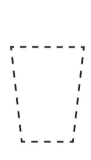 to show this number.

How many does Adam use?
Write the number.

© 2020 Marshall Cavendish Education Pte Ltd

© 2020 Marshall Cavendish Education Pte Ltd

1 Flat Shapes

LEARN Name flat shapes

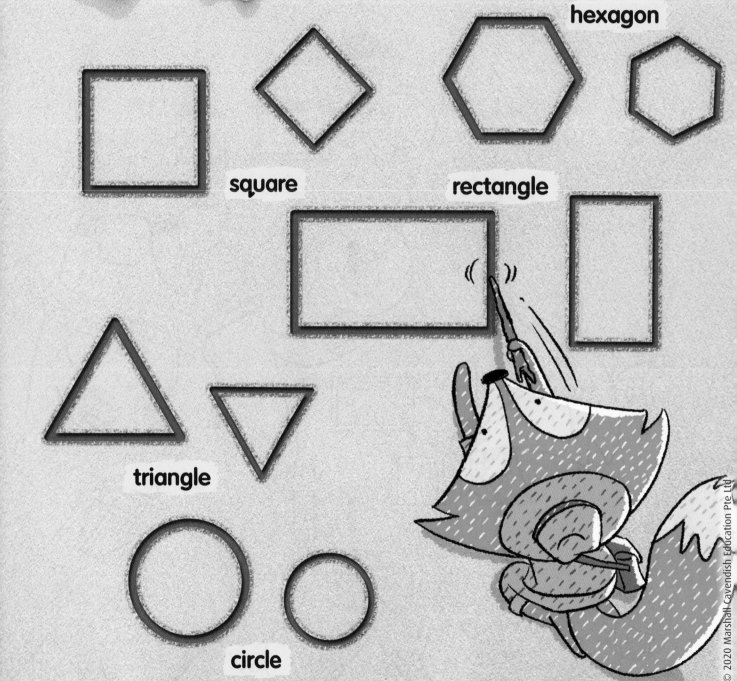

square

hexagon

rectangle

triangle

circle

© 2020 Marshall Cavendish Education Pte Ltd

TRY

Color each correct shape.

 1 rectangle

 2 triangle

3 hexagon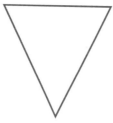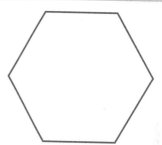

 4 circle

 5 square

© 2020 Marshall Cavendish Education Pte Ltd

Trace.
Color the box with the name of the shapes.

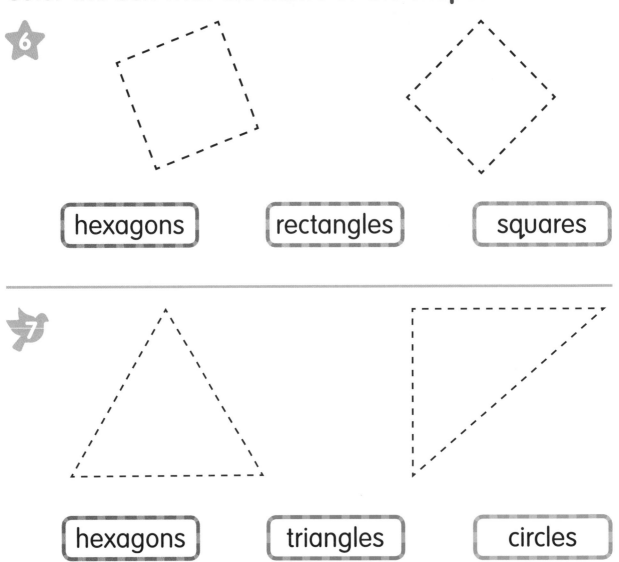

6

| hexagons | rectangles | squares |

7

| hexagons | triangles | circles |

© 2020 Marshall Cavendish Education Pte Ltd

8

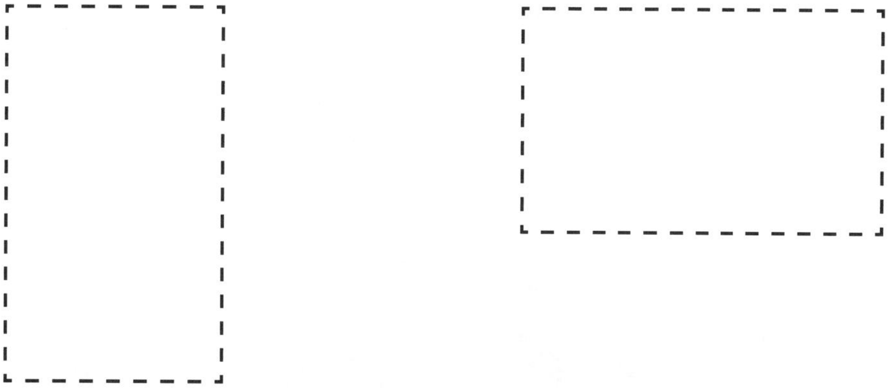

triangles · rectangles · squares

9

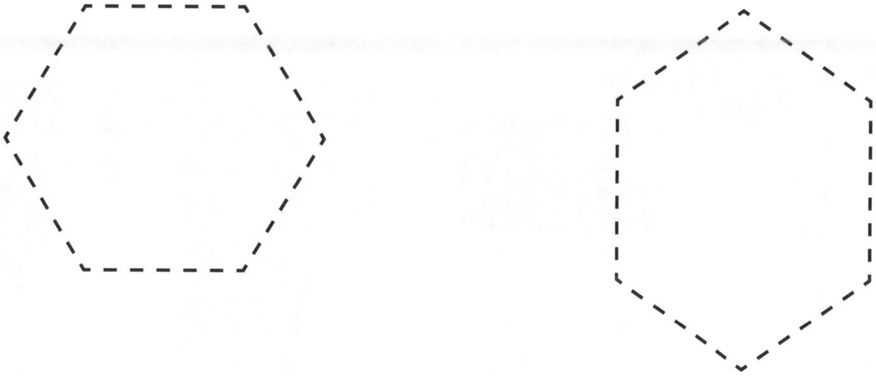

hexagons · triangles · circles

10

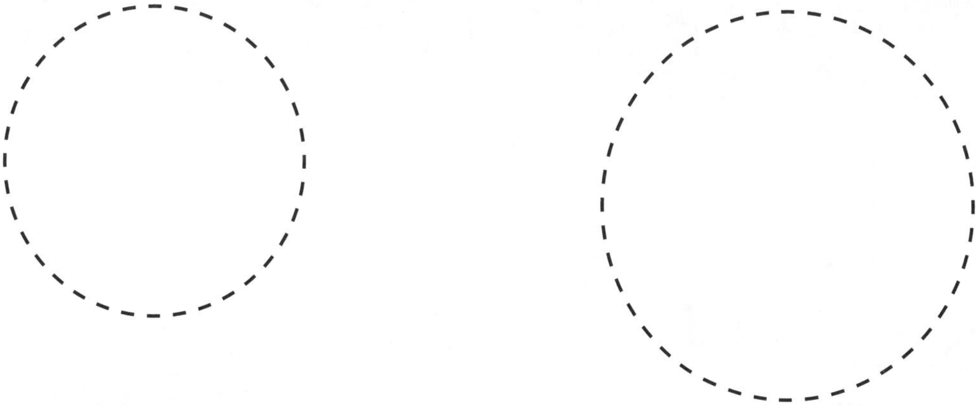

hexagons · circles · squares

© 2020 Marshall Cavendish Education Pte Ltd

© 2020 Marshall Cavendish Education Pte Ltd

TRY

Circle the shapes that are the same in each row.

 1

 2

 3

© 2020 Marshall Cavendish Education Pte Ltd

 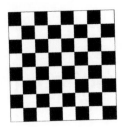 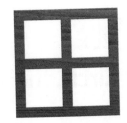

Circle the pictures that have triangles.

© 2020 Marshall Cavendish Education Pte Ltd

PRACTICE

Color each correct shape.

 1   square

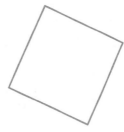 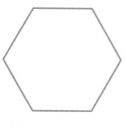

 2   hexagon

Look for a picture with each shape.
Then, draw the picture.

3   triangle

 4   rectangle

© 2020 Marshall Cavendish Education Pte Ltd

Which flat shape is it?
Color.

5

yellow   red   blue   orange   green

© 2020 Marshall Cavendish Education Pte Ltd

Name: _____ Date: _____

2 Solid Shapes

LEARN Name solid shapes

cube　　　**cylinder**　　　**cone**　　　**sphere**

TRY

Color each correct shape.

 1 │ cube │

---

 2 │ cone │

---

 3 │ sphere │

---

 4 │ cylinder │

© 2020 Marshall Cavendish Education Pte Ltd

Color the box with the name of the shapes.

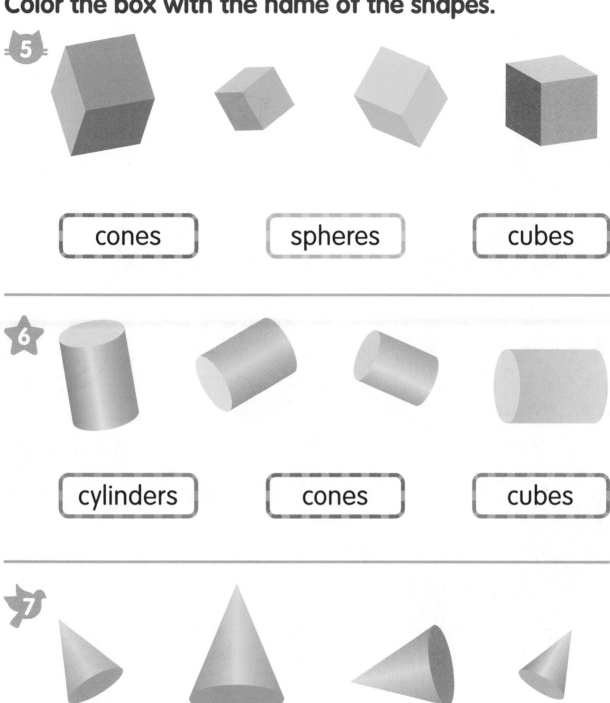

5

| cones | spheres | cubes |

6

| cylinders | cones | cubes |

7

| cylinders | cones | spheres |

© 2020 Marshall Cavendish Education Pte Ltd

© 2020 Marshall Cavendish Education Pte Ltd

TRY

Color the shapes that are the same in each row.

   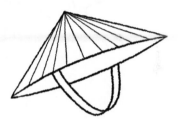

   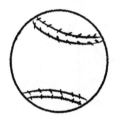 

© 2020 Marshall Cavendish Education Pte Ltd

LEARN Roll, slide, and stack

© 2020 Marshall Cavendish Education Pte Ltd

TRY

Circle.

 1 Which shape(s) can slide?

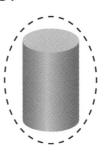

 **2** Which shape(s) can roll?

 3 Which shape(s) can both slide and roll?

2 Solid Shapes **247**

© 2020 Marshall Cavendish Education Pte Ltd

4 Which shape(s) can stack on themselves?

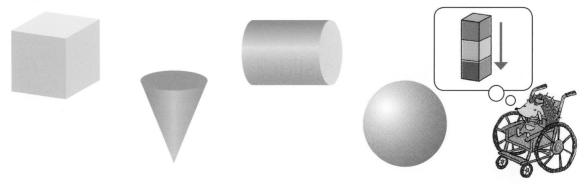

5 Which shape(s) can stack on other shapes?

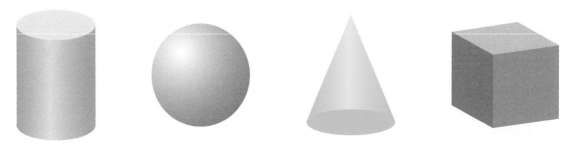

6 Which shape(s) can both roll and stack on themselves?

© 2020 Marshall Cavendish Education Pte Ltd

PRACTICE

Match.

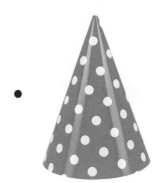

© 2020 Marshall Cavendish Education Pte Ltd

Which solid shape is it?
Color.

2

red   green   orange   blue

© 2020 Marshall Cavendish Education Pte Ltd

Which can roll?
Color them.
Which can slide?
Circle them.

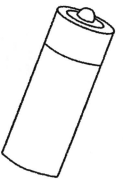

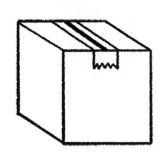

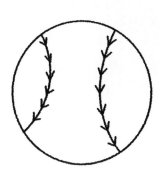

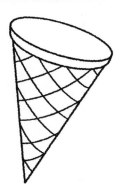

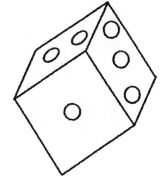

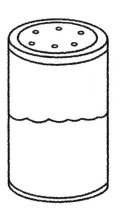

© 2020 Marshall Cavendish Education Pte Ltd

Which can slide and stack on themselves?
Circle them.

 4

© 2020 Marshall Cavendish Education Pte Ltd

© 2020 Marshall Cavendish Education Pte Ltd

Name: _____ Date: _____

3 Positions

LEARN Use position words

below

behind

above

next to

in front of

beside

Circle.

 1 What is **above** the ?

What is its shape?   circle   cube

---

 2 What is **behind** the ?

What is its shape?   hexagon   cylinder

---

 3 What is **beside** the ?

What is its shape?   cube   sphere

© 2020 Marshall Cavendish Education Pte Ltd

Circle.

© 2020 Marshall Cavendish Education Pte Ltd

 What is **in front of** the ?

What is its shape?   triangle   square

 What is **below** the ?

What is its shape?   square   cylinder

 What is **next to**
the ?

What is its shape?   triangle   square

Your teacher will give you some pictures.
Read the clues.
Paste the pictures.
Tell the shapes.

7

The ⌂ is behind the 🗑.

The ▯ is beside the ⊞.

The ▦ is in front of the 🌺🌺.

© 2020 Marshall Cavendish Education Pte Ltd

© 2020 Marshall Cavendish Education Pte Ltd

Name: _____ Date: _____

PRACTICE

Draw the object.
Color the correct box.

 Draw a below the .

What is its shape?

square
sphere

 Draw a in front of the .

What is its shape?

rectangle
cube

Look at the picture.

3 What is behind the 🎾?
Circle it.
Color the name of the shape.

cylinder
cube

4 What is above the 📦?
Make an **✗**.
Color the name of the shape.

square
circle

5 What is next to the 🎉?
Draw a box around it.
Color the name of the shape.

cube
sphere

© 2020 Marshall Cavendish Education Pte Ltd

4 Make New Shapes

LEARN Use flat shapes to make new shapes

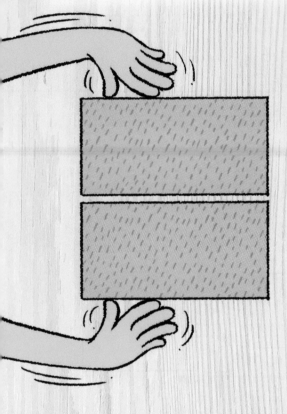

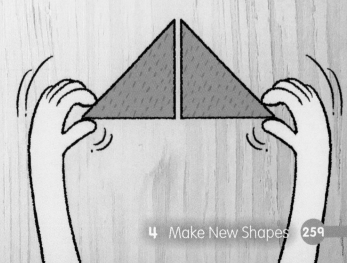

© 2020 Marshall Cavendish Education Pte Ltd

Use to make each shape.
Color the shapes you used.

1

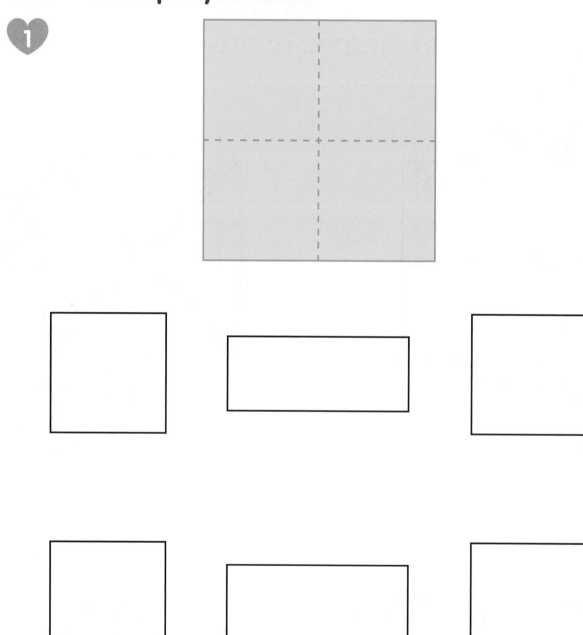

© 2020 Marshall Cavendish Education Pte Ltd

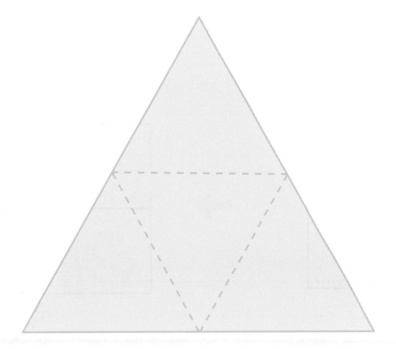

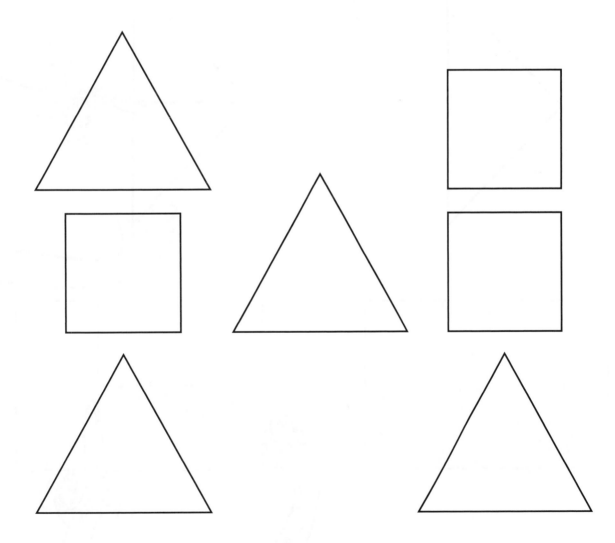

© 2020 Marshall Cavendish Education Pte Ltd

© 2020 Marshall Cavendish Education Pte Ltd

Your teacher will give you two hexagons.
Cut each hexagon to make the shapes given.
Draw lines to show how you make them.

 6 △

 2 ▭ and 2 △

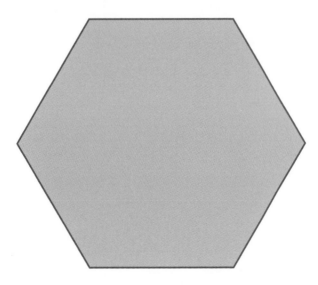

© 2020 Marshall Cavendish Education Pte Ltd

Your teacher will give you three rectangles.
Cut each rectangle into smaller shapes.
Draw lines to show how you did it.

3

© 2020 Marshall Cavendish Education Pte Ltd

Your teacher will give you three squares.
Cut each square into smaller shapes.
Draw lines to show how you did it.

© 2020 Marshall Cavendish Education Pte Ltd

© 2020 Marshall Cavendish Education Pte Ltd

TRY

Count.
Fill in each blank.

 1

rectangle	
square	
circle	
triangle	

2

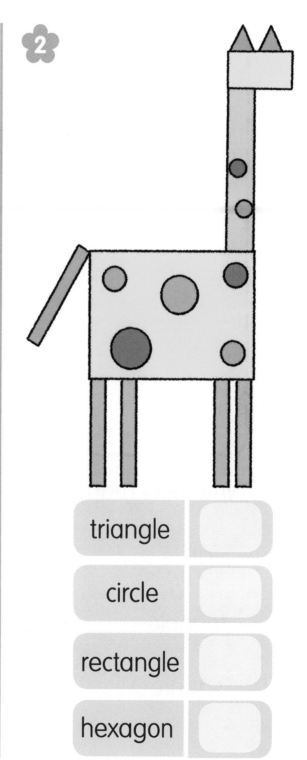

triangle	
circle	
rectangle	
hexagon	

© 2020 Marshall Cavendish Education Pte Ltd

Use shapes to draw a picture.

 3

Write how many of each shape you draw.

 circle [ ]

rectangle [ ]

triangle [ ]

hexagon [ ]

square [ ]

© 2020 Marshall Cavendish Education Pte Ltd

© 2020 Marshall Cavendish Education Pte Ltd

Count.
Fill in each blank.

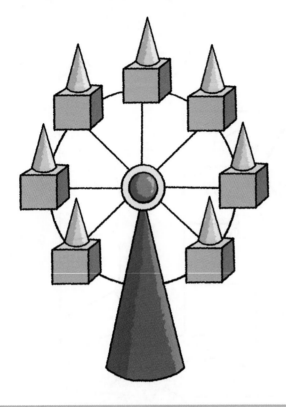

© 2020 Marshall Cavendish Education Pte Ltd

Name: _____   Date: _____

PRACTICE

Color the correct number of shapes.

1 What shapes make this square?

 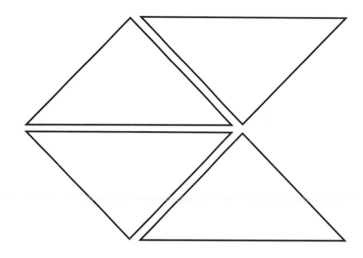

Draw lines to show how you make the shapes shown.

 4 ▢

© 2020 Marshall Cavendish Education Pte Ltd

2

---

4 4

© 2020 Marshall Cavendish Education Pte Ltd

1 ▭ and 2 ▭

Color the triangles red.
Color the hexagons blue.
Color the squares yellow.

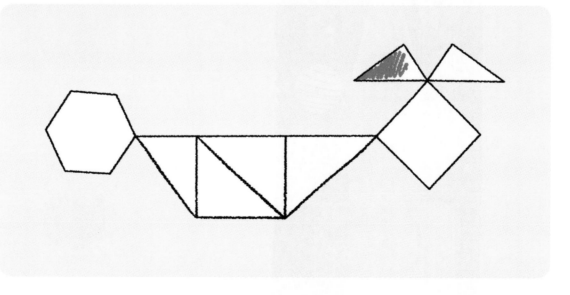

© 2020 Marshall Cavendish Education Pte Ltd

Count.
Fill in each blank.

 7

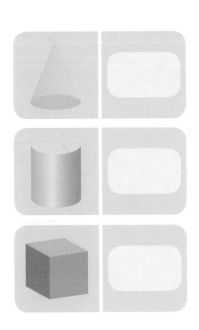

 8

© 2020 Marshall Cavendish Education Pte Ltd

© 2020 Marshall Cavendish Education Pte Ltd

Name: _____ Date: _____

5 Compare Flat and Solid Shapes

LEARN Compare flat shapes

TRY

Color the correct box to complete each sentence.

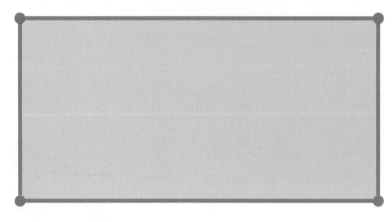

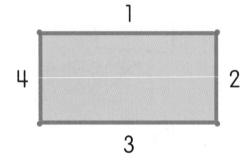

A rectangle has [2 | 3 | **4**] sides.

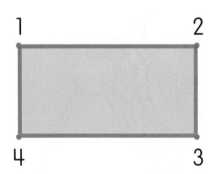

A rectangle has [2 | 3 | 4] corners.

© 2020 Marshall Cavendish Education Pte Ltd

2

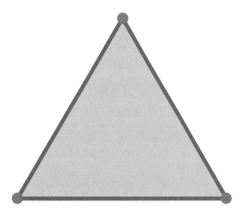

A triangle has | 2 | 3 | 4 | sides.

A triangle has | 2 | 3 | 4 | corners.

3

A square has | 2 | 3 | 4 | sides.

A square has | 2 | 3 | 4 | corners.

© 2020 Marshall Cavendish Education Pte Ltd

4

A hexagon has [4 | 6 | 8] sides.

A hexagon has [4 | 6 | 8] corners.

Draw.

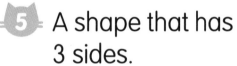 **5** A shape that has 3 sides.

6 A shape that has 4 sides.

© 2020 Marshall Cavendish Education Pte Ltd

Circle shapes with 3 corners.
Color shapes with 6 sides yellow.
Color shapes with 4 sides blue.

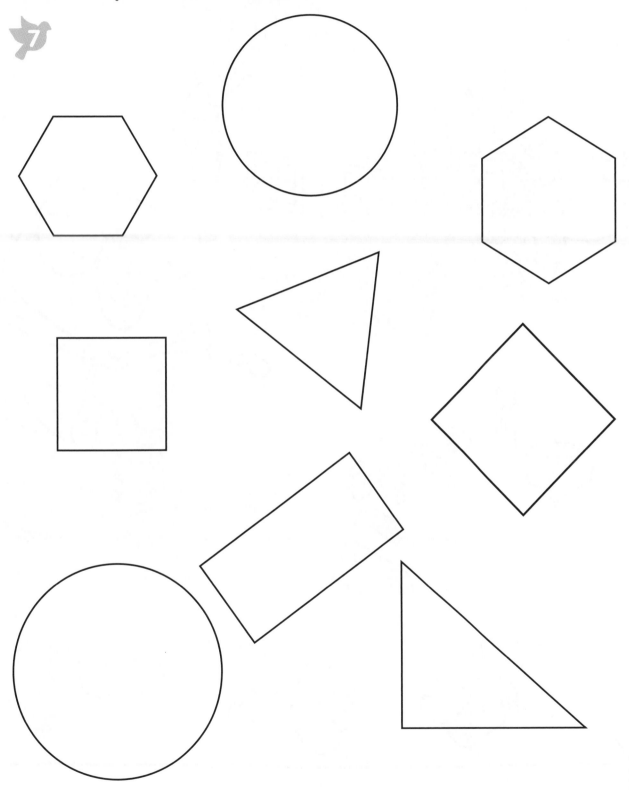

© 2020 Marshall Cavendish Education Pte Ltd

© 2020 Marshall Cavendish Education Pte Ltd

Circle.

 Which shapes have a curved surface?

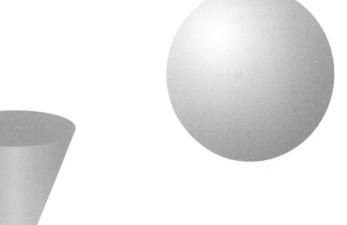

Shapes with curved surfaces can roll.

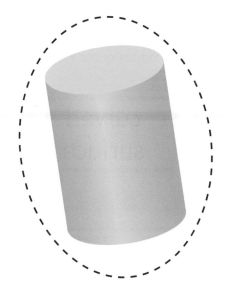

© 2020 Marshall Cavendish Education Pte Ltd

Which words describe each shape?
Color the boxes with these words.

flat face	curved surface

flat face	curved surface

flat face	curved surface

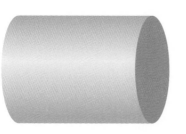

flat face	curved surface

© 2020 Marshall Cavendish Education Pte Ltd

PRACTICE

Color shapes with exactly 4 corners.

© 2020 Marshall Cavendish Education Pte Ltd

Color all flat shapes red.
Color all solid shapes blue.

© 2020 Marshall Cavendish Education Pte Ltd

6 Shape Patterns

LEARN Use shapes to look for patterns

© 2020 Marshall Cavendish Education Pte Ltd

TRY

Which set of shapes repeats?
Draw a box.

1

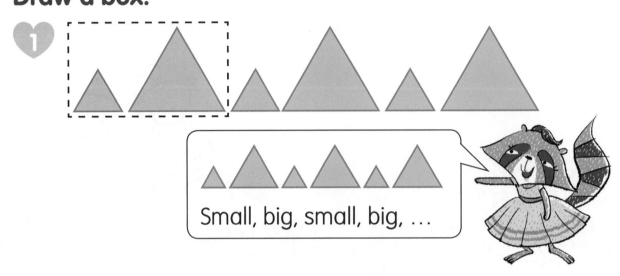

Small, big, small, big, …

2

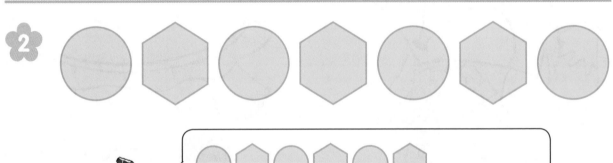

Circle, hexagon, circle, hexagon, …

3

© 2020 Marshall Cavendish Education Pte Ltd

What shape comes next?
Circle it.

4

5

6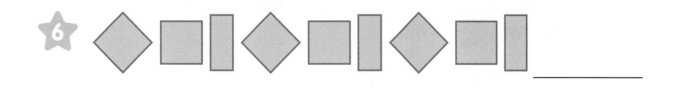

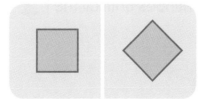

© 2020 Marshall Cavendish Education Pte Ltd

SNAP

What you need:

Players: 2

Materials: 1 set of

What to do:

1　Player 1 shuffles the 🔺 and distributes them equally.

2　Each player places his or her 🔺 in a stack face down. Turn a 🔺 over, one at a time. Place the 🔺 in the center. Say *snap* when two 🔺 match.

3　When two 🔺 match, the one who says *snap* first takes the pile of 🔺. The game continues until all the 🔺 have been turned over.

Who is the winner?

The player who has the most wins.

© 2020 Marshall Cavendish Education Pte Ltd

PRACTICE

What is the missing shape?
Color it.

 1

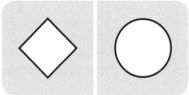

2

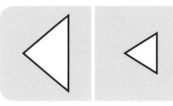

3

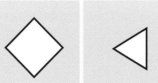

© 2020 Marshall Cavendish Education Pte Ltd

What is the missing shape?
Circle it.

4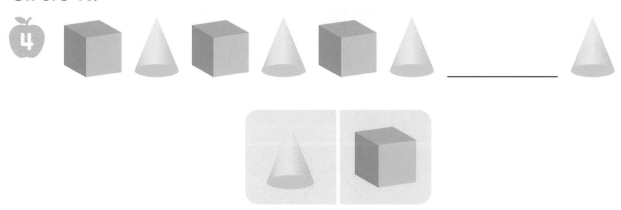

5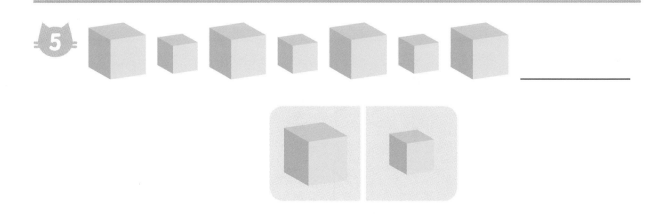

6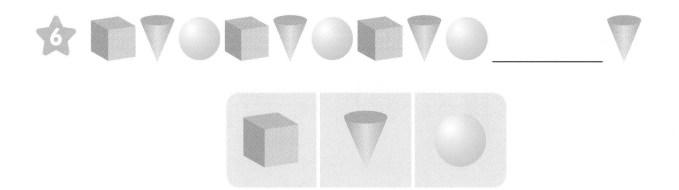

© 2020 Marshall Cavendish Education Pte Ltd

Name: _____ Date: _____

1 David draws a flat shape.
It has 6 sides and 6 corners.
Circle the shape David draws.

Look for the flat shapes first.

2 Zoey has a solid shape.
It can slide and roll.
It has one flat face.
Circle the shape Zoey has.

Which shape(s) can slide and roll?

3 Arrange the shapes to make a pattern.
Draw them in the box.

© 2020 Marshall Cavendish Education Pte Ltd

MY MATH DICTIONARY

Flat shapes

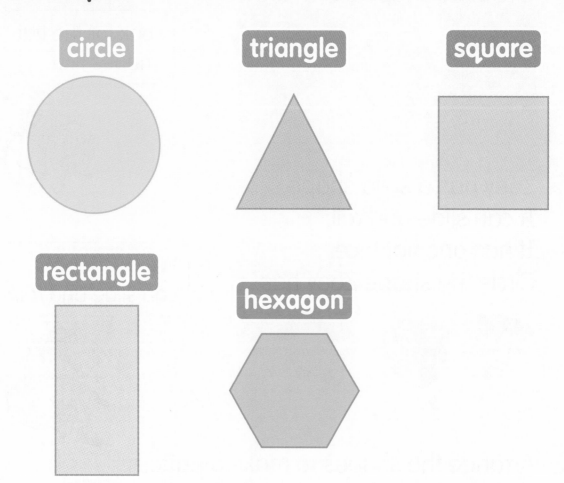

circle

triangle

square

rectangle

hexagon

Solid shapes

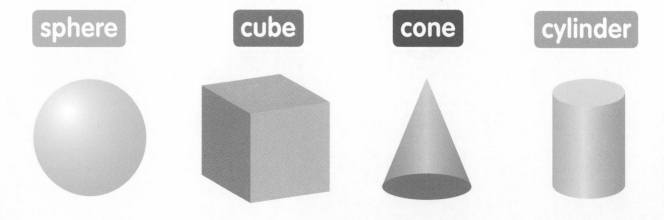

sphere

cube

cone

cylinder

© 2020 Marshall Cavendish Education Pte Ltd

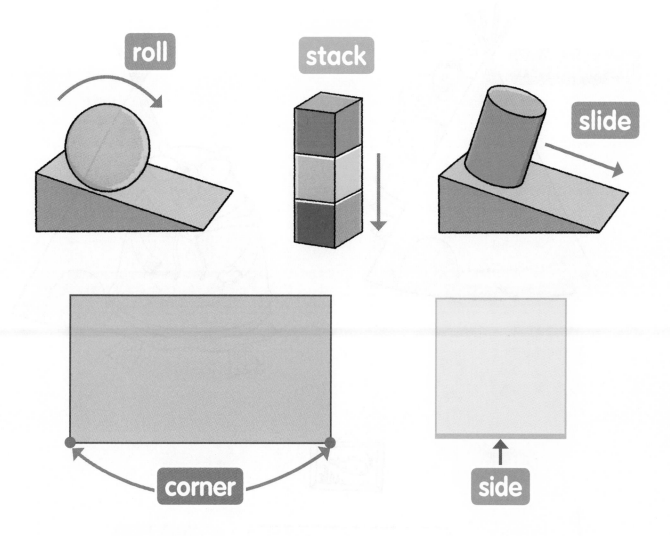

roll

stack

slide

corner

side

Spheres, cones,
and cylinders have
curved surfaces.

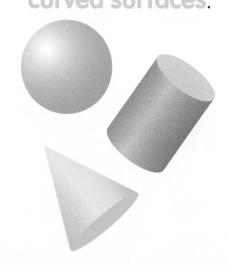

Cubes, cylinders,
and cones have
flat faces.

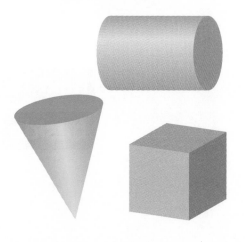

© 2020 Marshall Cavendish Education Pte Ltd

in front of

behind

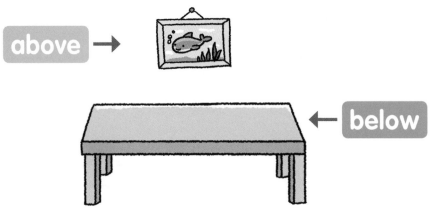

above

below

next to
beside

© 2020 Marshall Cavendish Education Pte Ltd

Name: _____ Date: _____

Trace each picture.
Color each correct word.

 1

triangle

circle   square

 2

rectangle

square   hexagon

 3

triangle

rectangle   hexagon

© 2020 Marshall Cavendish Education Pte Ltd

Match.

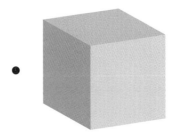

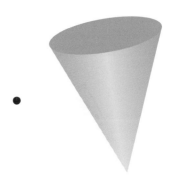

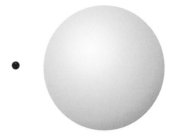

© 2020 Marshall Cavendish Education Pte Ltd

Circle.

 5 Which shape(s) can roll?

---

 6 Which shape(s) can stack on themselves?

---

 7 Which shape(s) can slide?

© 2020 Marshall Cavendish Education Pte Ltd

Look at the picture.

8 What is **in front of** the ◢▱◣?
Circle it.
Circle the name of the shape. [cube] [cylinder]

9 What is **behind** the ⬱?
Make an ✗ on it.
Circle the name of the shape. [sphere] [cone]

10 What is **beside** the ⬱?
Draw a box around it.
Circle the name of the shape. [square] [circle]

© 2020 Marshall Cavendish Education Pte Ltd

Draw lines to make 2 ▢ and 2 ◺.

11

Count.
Fill in each blank.

12

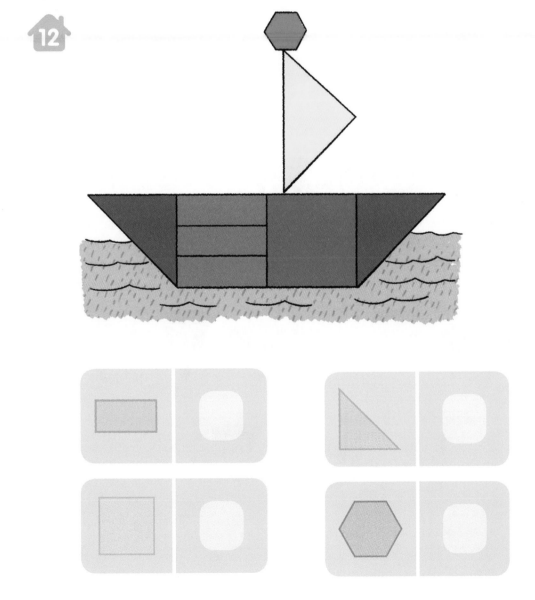

© 2020 Marshall Cavendish Education Pte Ltd

What shape comes next?
Circle it.

13

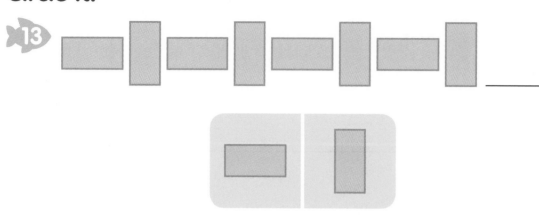

14

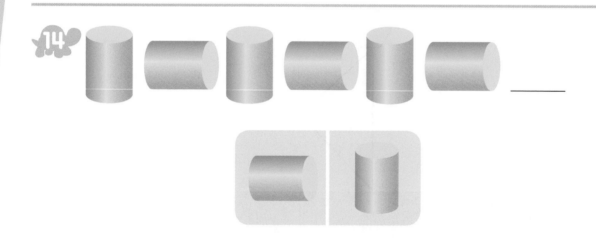

15

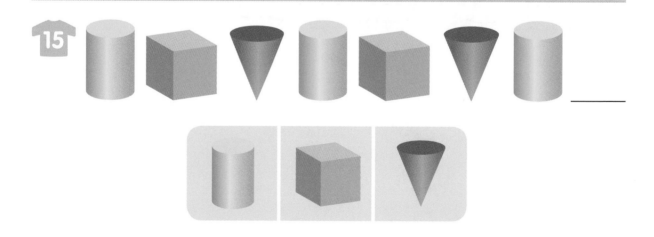

© 2020 Marshall Cavendish Education Pte Ltd

Assessment Prep
Answer each question.

 Color the shapes with 6 sides.

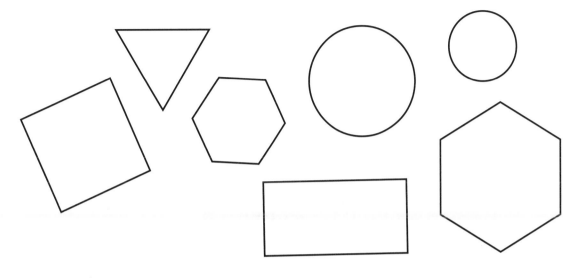

 Which shapes have a curved surface?
Circle them.

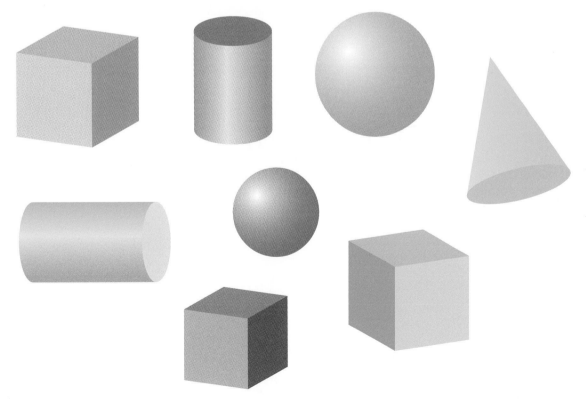

© 2020 Marshall Cavendish Education Pte Ltd

18 Which shapes make a square?

Circle the groups.

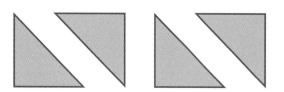

© 2020 Marshall Cavendish Education Pte Ltd

Name: _____   Date: _____

Craft Time
How many ways can you make a triangle?
Trace the shapes.

 Use 4 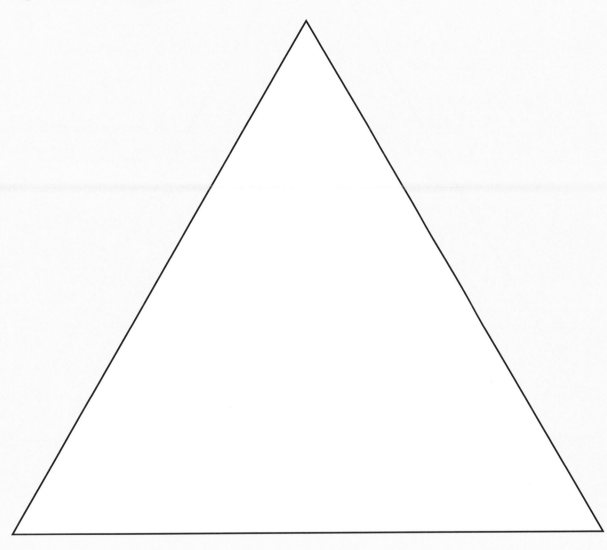.

© 2020 Marshall Cavendish Education Pte Ltd

Use 1 and 3 .

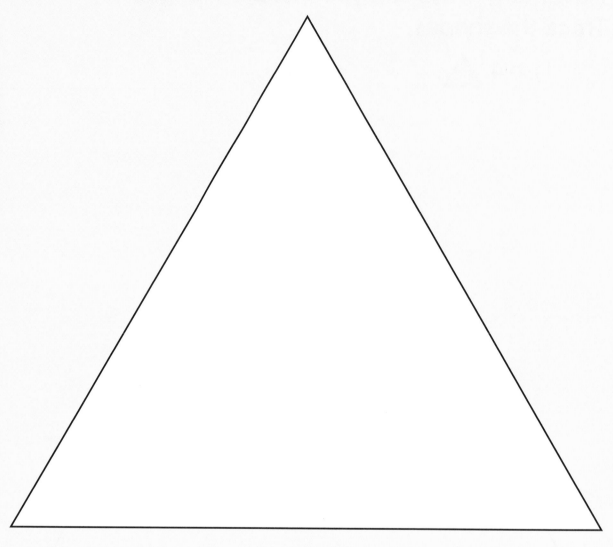

© 2020 Marshall Cavendish Education Pte Ltd

Use 9 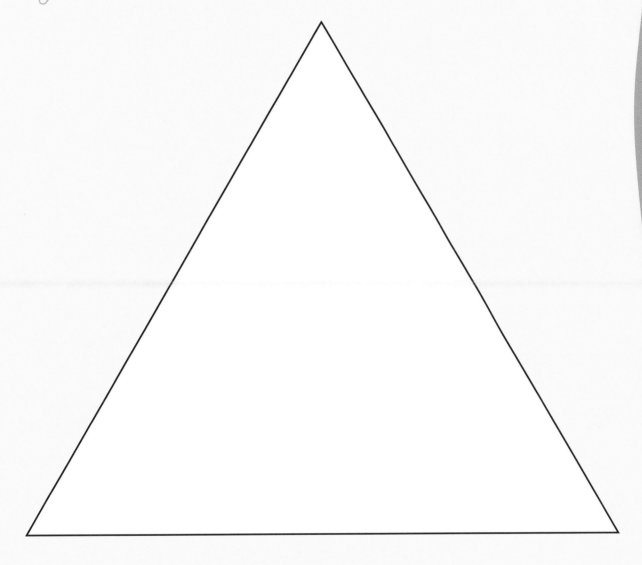.

© 2020 Marshall Cavendish Education Pte Ltd

Make a square.

 Use exactly 4 to make a big square.
Trace the shape.

How many of each shape do you use?

square

hexagon

rectangle

© 2020 Marshall Cavendish Education Pte Ltd

Glossary

A

- **above**

- **as heavy as**

- **as long as**

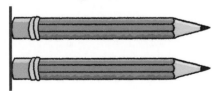

- **as tall as**

B

- **behind**

© 2020 Marshall Cavendish Education Pte Ltd

below

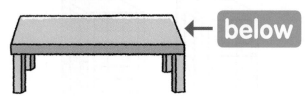

beside

circle

cone

corner

© 2020 Marshall Cavendish Education Pte Ltd

- **cube**

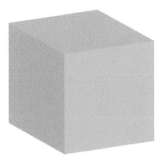

- **curved surface**

Spheres, cones, and cylinders have curved surfaces.

- **cylinder**

- **eight**

Count	Number	Word
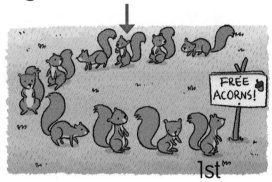	8	eight

- **eighth**

- **fewer than**

There are fewer 🪹 than 🐔.

© 2020 Marshall Cavendish Education Pte Ltd

fifth

first

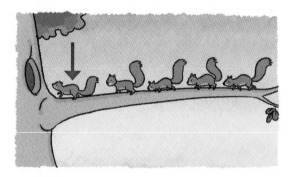

five

Count	Number	Word
	5	five

flat face

Cones, cylinders, and cubes have flat faces.

flat shapes

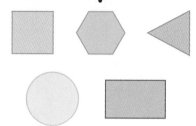

four

Count	Number	Word
	4	four

fourth

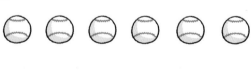

greater than

6 is greater than 4.

© 2020 Marshall Cavendish Education Pte Ltd

H

- **heavier**

← heavier

- **hexagon**

I

- **in front of**

in front of →

L

- **1 less**

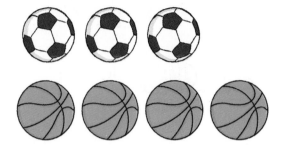

1 less than 4 is 3.
3 is 1 less than 4.

- **less than**

3 is less than 5.

- **lighter**

↑
lighter

© 2020 Marshall Cavendish Education Pte Ltd

longer

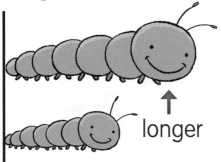

longer

M

1 more

1 more than 4 is 5.
5 is 1 more than 4.

more than

There are more 🌹 than
🌸.

N

next to

next to

nine

Count	Number	Word
	9	nine

ninth

number pair

2 and 3 make 5.

© 2020 Marshall Cavendish Education Pte Ltd

O

one

Count	Number	Word
	1	one

R

rectangle

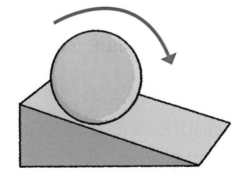

roll

A sphere can roll.

same

the same number of muffins

same height

The two rockets have the same height.

same length

The ruler and the paintbrush have the same length.

© 2020 Marshall Cavendish Education Pte Ltd

same weight

The two bells have the same weight.

second

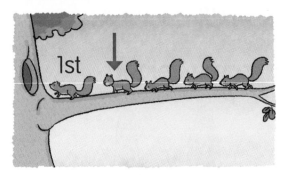

1st

seven

Count	Number	Word
	7	seven

seventh

FREE ACORNS!

1st

shorter

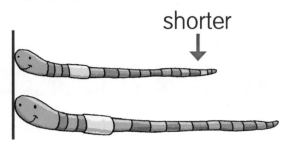

shorter

shorter

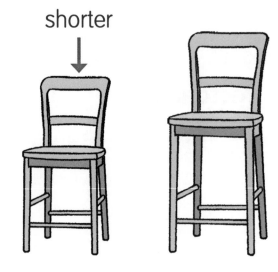

side

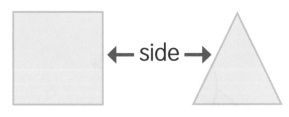

← side →

A square has 4 sides.
A triangle has 3 sides.

six

Count	Number	Word
	6	six

© 2020 Marshall Cavendish Education Pte Ltd

sixth

slide

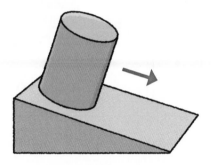

A cylinder can slide.

solid shapes

sphere

square

stack

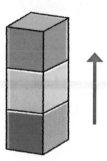

Cubes can stack.

T

taller

taller

© 2020 Marshall Cavendish Education Pte Ltd

ten

Count	Number	Word
(ten-frame with 10 filled)	10	ten

tenth

third

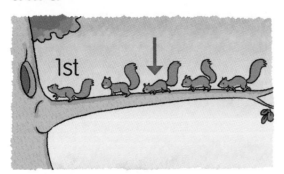

three

Count	Number	Word
(ten-frame with 3 filled)	3	three

triangle

two

Count	Number	Word
(ten-frame with 2 filled)	2	two

Z

zero

Count	Number	Word
(empty ten-frame)	0	zero

© 2020 Marshall Cavendish Education Pte Ltd

Photo Credits

1: © janniwet/Think Stock/iStock, 1tm: © Hayati Kayhan/Shutter Stock, 1ml: © philipus/123rf.com, 1mm: © serezniy/123rf.com, 1mr: © Viktor Prymachenk/Dreamstime.com, 1b: © Kittaya Mangruan/123rf.com, 1b: © RusN/Think Stock/iStock, 1bm: © Natalia Pauk/123rf.com, 2: © janniwet/Think Stock/iStock, 2tl: © watin/Shutter Stock, 4tl: © jirkaejc/Think Stock/iStock, 11: © andresusK/Think Stock/iStock, 11m: © pkanchana/Think Stock/iStock, 11b: © donatas1205/Shutter Stock, 13(tl to bl): i) © lior2/Think Stock/iStock, ii) © Zoonar/Think Stock/iStock, iii) © Timmary/123rf.com, iv) © patpitchaya/Shutter Stock, 15tl: © Azure-Dragon/Think Stock/iStock, 15tr: © Lunglee5458/Dreamstime.com, 15bl: © Nikolai Sorokin/Dreamstime.com, 15br: © alekss/123rf.com, 16(tl to bl): i) © Alexei Novikov/Dreamstime.com, ii) Irogova/Dreamstime.com, iii) © Irogova3/Dreamstime.com, iv) © Irogova/Dreamstime.com, 18t: © MCE, 21: © poligonchik/Think Stock/iStock, 21br: © Anthony Paz – Photographer/Think Stock/iStock, 24t: © Ksena2009/Dreamstime.com, 29: © Anna Andersson Fotografi/Shutter Stock, 29b: © photka/Shutter Stock, 35: © Tirachard/Think Stock/iStock, 38: © piotr_pabijan/Shutter Stock, 46b: © WolfeLarry/Think Stock/iStock, 49: © Phanuwat Nandee/123rf.com, 49t: © ryoota/Think Stock/iStock, 49ml: © Jumini Jumini/123rf.com, 49bl: © nalin chanthorn/Shutter Stock, 49br: © S-S-S/Think Stock/iStock, 50: © baona/iStock, 51: © design56/Think Stock/iStock, 52tl: ©MCE, 53: © Charles Brutlag/123rf.com, 56 © Akapelux/Dreamstime.com, 56ml: © Elvira Gomolach/123rf.com, 57: © tiero/123rf.com, 65: © Ksw Photographer/Shutter Stock, 65m: © rangizzz/Shutter Stock, 65mr: © Alex Emanuel Koch/Sutter Stock, 65br: © lleerogers/iStock, 66tl: ©MCE, 71: © Ksw Photographer/Shutter Stock, 71tl: © bobrik74/Think Stock/iStock, 71tr: © alekss/123rf.com, 72l: © bobrik74/Think Stock/iStock, 73tl: ©MCE, 73t: © ronniechua/Think Stock/iStock, 73m: © Ekkapon/Think Stock/iStock, 73b: © lleerogers/iStock, 75t: © Alexstar/Dreamstime.com. 75m: © egal/Think Stock/iStock, 75b: © piovesempre/Think Stock/iStock, 81m: © BALDARI/iStock, 81m: © Es sarawuth/Shutter Stock, 81m: © photobalance/123rf.com, 81b: © All For You/Shutter Stock, 83tl: © MCE, 83t: © Yocamon/Think Stock/iStock, 83m: © fckncg/123rf.com. 83b: © Jmad/Dreamstime.com, 84t: © Tikkirio/Dreamstime.com, 89: © Vlue/Shutter Stock, 89m: © Maksim

Borzdov/123rf.com, 93: © Pavlo Vakhrushev/Dreamstime.com, 96t: © MCE, 97t: © MCE, 98: © Themorningglory/Dreamstime.com, 101: © Pavlo Vakhrushev/Dreamstime.com, 104: © ELENA POLINA/123rf.com, 109: © tcharts/Shutter Stock, 109tl: © rSnapshotPhotos/Shutter Stock, 112: © piotr_pabijan/Shutter Stock, 112: © MCE. Objects sponsored by Noble International Pte Ltd., 116b: © MCE, 117: © Natali_Giglavaya/Shutter Stock, 124bl: © MCE, 125: © jorgeyu at Morguefile.com, 125tl: aconant at Morguefile.com, 125tr: © Jusben at Morguefile.com, 125m: © Szabolcs Stieber/Dreamstime.com, 125br: © talldude07 at Morguefile.com, 126t: © Softlightaa/Dreamstime.com, 126b: © Avesun/Dreamstime.com, 132: © Oleg Beloborodov/123rf.com, 132m: © mtsaride/123rf.com, 132m: © Geopappas/Dreamstime.com, 132b: © kritchanut/123rf.com, 133: © MCE. Objects sponsored by Noble International Pte Ltd., 134: © Geopappas/Dreamstime.com, 135: © natrot/Shutter Stock, 135tl: © rSnapshotPhotos/Shutter Stock, 135ml: © pioneer111/Think Stock/iStock, 135bl: © rSnapshotPhotos/Shutter Stock, 135bm: © pioneer111/Think Stock/iStock, 136t: © MCE. Objects sponsored by Noble International Pte Ltd., 136t: © Houghton Mifflin Harcourt, 136(ml to bl): i) © Youry Ermoshkin/123rf.com. ii) © Andregric/iStock, iii) © Yana Gulyanovska/Dreamstime.com, 139(t to b): i) © Dumrongsak Songdej/Dreamstime.com, ii) © mtsaride/123rf.com, iii) Arthur Mustafa/Shutter Stock, 140: © natrot/Shutter Stock, 140t: © Nilsz/Dreamstime.com, 140b: © prapann/Shutter Stock, 141: © KobchaiMa/Shutter Stock, 146mr: © Alexander Tolstykh/123rf.com, 146bl: © Alexander Tolstykh/123rf.com, 146bm: © Georgina198/Shutter Stock, 146br: © KayaMe/Shutter Stock, 147: © Tr1sha/Shutter Stock, 147tl: © photka/Shutter Stock, 147(t to m): © Dannyphoto80/Dreamstime.com, 147b: © Anthony Paz – Photographer/Think Stock/iStock, 147bm: © MCE. Objects sponsored by Noble International Pte Ltd., 148: © MCE. Objects sponsored by Noble International Pte Ltd., 149: © MCE. Objects sponsored by Noble International Pte Ltd., 149(tl to ml): i) © Plasticrobot/Dreamstime.com, ii) © Tatyana Vychegzhanina/Dreamstime.com, iii) © Plasticrobot/Dreamstime.com, iv) © Tatyana Vychegzhanina/Dreamstime.com, v) © Scruggelgreen/Dreamstime.com, 149tm: © Scruggelgreen/Dreamstime.com, 149(bl to br): i) © Plasticrobot/Dreamstime.com,

© 2020 Marshall Cavendish Education Pte Ltd

ii) © Tatyana Vychegzhanina/Dreamstime.com,
iii) © Tatyana Vychegzhanina/Dreamstime.com,
iv) © Scruggelgreen/Dreamstime.com, 150t:
© MCE. Objects sponsored by Noble International
Pte Ltd., 150t: © Dannyphoto80/Dreamstime.com,
150(ml to bl): i) © Sarawut Chainawarat/Dreamstime.
com, ii) © dhanaji/123rf.com, iii) © Christian
Delbert/123rf.com, 153: © MCE. Objects sponsored
by Noble International Pte Ltd., 153tl: © area381/
Shutter Stock, 153ml: © lucadp/123rf.com,
153bm: © Dannyphoto80/Dreamstime.com,
154: © Dannyphoto80/Dreamstime.com,
154tl: © Irogova/Dreamstime.com, 154ml:
© Tammajak Payom/123rf.com, 154bl: © Alexander
Tolstykh/Dreamstime.com, 155(mm to mr):
i) © Irogova3/Dreamstime.com, ii): © Yocamon/
Think Stock/iStock, iii) © Elphotographo/Dreamstime.
com, 155(bl to br): i) © Hongmai2012/Dreamstime.
com, ii) © Arthur Mustafa/Shutter Stock, iii) © Stepan
Bormotov/123rf.com, iv) © Alexstar/Dreamstime.
com, 156tl: © natee trireaklith/123rf.com, 156tr:
© Elena Schweitzer/Dreamstime.com, 156ml:
© Phive2015/Dreamstime.com, 156mr:
© Witoon Buttre/Dreamstime.com, 156bl:
© Olga Popova/123rf.com, 156br: © Jiri Miklo/123rf.
com, 157tl: © Sergiy Kalugin/Dreamstime.com, 157tr:
© Sharpshot/Dreamstime.com, 157ml: © Kevin
Mayer/123rf.com, 157mr: © pixelrobot/123rf.com,
157bl: © jikkoh/123rf.com, 157br: © urfin/Shutter
Stock, 158tl: © Szerdahelyi Adam/Dreamstime.com,
158tr: © Patryk Kosmider/Dreamstime.com,
158m: © Severija/Dreamstime.com, 158bl:
© Py2000/Dreamstime.com, 158br: © Stargatechris/
Dreamstime.com, 159: © Anna Andersson Fotografi/
Shutter Stock, 159b: © kritchanut/123rf.com, 160tl:
© Maksym Yemelyanov/123rf.com, 160tr:
© Andrii Klemenchenko/Dreamstime.com, 160ml:
© Timmary/123rf.com, 160mr: © Alexstar/
Dreamstime.com, 160bl: © Sirirat Savettanant/
Dreamstime.com, 160br:
© Yastrebinsky/Dreamstime.com, 162: © pioneer111/
Think Stock/iStock, 162: © Akiyoko74/Dreamstime.
com, 163: © Scruggelgreen/Dreamstime.com,
163; © Chalermpon/Dreamstime.com, 164:
© piotr_pabijan/Shutter Stock, 165tl: © Kpmvsk11/
Dreamstime.com, 165tr: © Stepan Bormotov/123rf.
com, 165ml: © Pavel Ignatov/123rf.com, 165mr:
© Stargatechris/Dreamstime.com, 165bl: © Ivan
Zhurov/Dreamstime.com, 165br: © Alexander
Tolstykh/123rf.com, 166tl: © nerthuz/123rf.com,
166tr: © Choochat Kaksup/Dreamstime.com, 166ml:
© Koleg68/Dreamstime.com, 166mr: © Dmitriy
Moroz/Dreamstime.com, 166bl: © Apolobay/
Dreamstime.com, 166br: © Marusea Turcu/
Dreamstime.com, 167tl: © Sergey Rusako/

Dreamstime.com, 167tr: © Chatcameraman/
Dreamstime.com, 167ml: © Godruma/Dreamstime.
com, 167mr: © Duncan Noakes/Dreamstime.com,
167bl: © Oleg Dudko/Dreamstime.com, 167br:
© Johnfoto/Dreamstime.com,
168tr: © tiero/123rf.com, 168tl: © alekss/123rf.com,
168tm: © tiero/123rf.com, 168tr: © cosmin4000/Think
Stock/iStock, 168ml: © krishh/Think Stock/iStock,
168mr: © Aleksander Ugorenkov/Dreamstime.com,
171: © Geopappas/Dreamstime.com, 171: © natrot/
Shutter Stock, 173(t to m): i) © Axstokes/Dreamstime.
com, ii) © Youry Ermoshkin/123rf.com,
iii) © Yellow Cat/Shutter Stock, 173bl:
© Scruggelgreen/Dreamstime.com, 173br:
© MsMaria/Shutter Stock, 174t: © AzriSuratmin/
Shutter Stock, 174ml: © Maffi/Shutter Stock,
174mr: © Nikanovak/Dreamstime.com, 176t:
© Geopappas/Dreamstime.com, 176t:
© Fotoplanner/Dreamstime.com, 176(m to b):
© natrot/Shutter Stock, 176m: © Наталья
Осканова/Dreamstime.com, 176b: © Drugoy66/
Dreamstime.com, 178: © MCE. Objects sponsored
by Nobel International Pte Ltd., 178tl: © Hurst Photo/
Shutter Stock, 178bl: © Chalermpon Poungpet/
Dreamstime.com, 179tl: © Yuri Bizgajmer/123rf.com,
179tr: © Valentyn75/Dreamstime.com, 179ml:
© Peleg Elkalay/Shutter Stock, 179mr:
© Dmitriy Moroz/Dreamstime.com, 179bl: © Cloki/
Dreamstime.com, 179br: © Alptraum/Dreamstime.
com, 183: © djgis/Shutter Stock, 183b: © Vixit/Shutter
Stock, 184: © andreusK/Think Stock/iStock, 188t:
© Aleksandr Ugorenkov/Dreamstime.com, 191t:
© Aedka Studio/Shutter Stock, 191b: © mathompl/
Think Stock/iStock, 199: © bazilfoto/Think Stock/
iStock, 199b: © Africa Studio/Shutter Stock, 205:
© jassada watt/Shutter Stock, 206: © Stas_V/
Think Stock/iStock, 206: © lleerogers/iStock, 209:
© strixcode/Think Stock/iStock, 211t: © Apolobay/
Dreamstime.com, 211m: © alekss/123rf.com, 214:
© piotr_pabijan/Shutter Stock, 214mr: © MCE.
Objects sponsored by Noble International Pte Ltd.,
220tl: © MCE, 226b: © Phive2015/Dreamstime.com,
231: © zsv3207/Think Stock/iStock, 231tl: © Oleg
Gapeenko/Dreamstime.com, 231tm: © Pupes/123rf.
com, 231(tm to tr): © Izonda/Dreamstime.com,
231bl: © imstock/Shutter Stock, 231br: © gorra/
Shutter Stock, 232: © Aliaksandr Mazurkevich/
Dreamstime.com, 236: © Irina88w/Dreamstime.
com, 236tm: © Ricochet69/Dreamstime.com,
236mr: © Darkcanuck/Dreamstime.com, 237tl:
© Heinteh/123rf.com, 237tm: © Eshmadeva/
Dreamstime.com, 237tr: © Ian Keirle/Dreamstime.
com, 237ml: © Natali_Giglavaya/Shutter Stock,
237mm: © Elisabeth Burrell/Dreamstime.com,
237mr: © Verdateo/Dreamstime.com, 237bl:

© Picsfive/123rf.com, 237bm: © Component/Shutter Stock, 237br: © Houghton Mifflin Harcourt, 238tl: © Belchonock/123rf.com, 238tm: © Vvoevale/Dreamstime.com, 238tr: © Romantiche/Dreamstime.com, 238ml: © Atipat Chantarak/Dreamstime.com, 238mm: © Goir/Dreamstime.com, 238mr: © Direk Takmatcha/Dreamstime.com, 241: © alhovik/123rf.com, 244: © Oleg Beloborodov/123rf.com, 244mm: © Mikhail Kokhanchikov/Dreamstime.com, 244bl: © Kpmvsk11/Dreamstime.com, 244bl: © gorra/Shutter Stock, 246: © Tr1sha/Shutter Stock, 246tm: © CHAIWATPHOTOS/Shutter Stock, 246tm: © PhilipYb Studio/Shutter Stock, 246bl: © gorra/Shutter Stock, 249(tr to br): i) © Kpmvsk11/Dreamstime.com, ii) © Petr Malyshev/Dreamstime.com, iii) © pixelrobot/123rf.com, iv) © Timmary/123rf.com, 252tl: © magraphics/123rf.com, 252tm: © Stepan Bormotov/123rf.com, 252tr: © Taa22/123rf.com, 252ml: © Georgii Dolgykh/123rf.com, 252mm: © pixelrobot/123rf.com, 252mr: © Cenkay Sahinalp/Dreamstime.com, 252bl: © Hshii/123rf.com, 252br: © Tashatuvango/123rf.com, 253: © khunaspix/123rf.com, 253: © Mikhail Mischenko/Shutter Stock, 253mm: © Mikhail Strogalev/Dreamstime.com, 253b: © donatas1205/Shutter Stock, 259: © Tihomir Trifonov/Dreamstime.com, 262: © Tihomir Trifonov/Dreamstime.com, 266: © Pressureua/Dreamstime.com, 266t: © picsfive/123rf.com, 266m: © Andrey Suslov/Shutter Stock, 269: © janniwet wangkiri/123rf.com, 274: © Irogova/Dreamstime.com, 275: © Stelmakh Oxana/Shutter Stock, 280: © Tr1sha/Shutter Stock, 280tm: © pixelrobot/123rf.com, 280mm: © Haveseen/Dreamstime.com, 285: © Oleg Beloborodv/123rf.com, 288: © piotr_pabijan/Shutter Stock, 295tl: © Ian Keirle/Dreamstime.com, 295ml: © Warut Chinsai/123rf.com, 295bl: © Nina Demianenko/123rf.com, 296(tl to bl): i) Stacy Barnett/Dreamstime.com, ii) Aldo Di Bari Murga/Dreamstime.com, iii) Peanutroaster/Dreamstime.com, iv) Andranik Tigranyan/Dreamstime.com

© 2020 Marshall Cavendish Education Pte Ltd

NOTES

NOTES

© 2020 Marshall Cavendish Education Pte Ltd

Published by Marshall Cavendish Education
Times Centre, 1 New Industrial Road, Singapore 536196
Customer Service Hotline: (65) 6213 9688
US Office Tel: (1-914) 332 8888 | Fax: (1-914) 332 8882
E-mail: cs@mceducation.com
Website: www.mceducation.com

Distributed by
Houghton Mifflin Harcourt
125 High Street
Boston, MA 02110
Tel: 617-351-5000
Website: www.hmhco.com/programs/math-in-focus

First published 2020

All rights reserved. No part of this publication may be reproduced, stored in a retrieval system or transmitted, in any form or by any means, electronic, mechanical, photocopying, recording or otherwise, without the prior written permission of Marshall Cavendish Education. If you have received these materials as examination copies free of charge, Marshall Cavendish Education retains the rights to the materials and they may not be resold. Resale of examination copies is strictly prohibited.

Marshall Cavendish® and *Math in Focus*® are registered trademarks of Times Publishing Limited.

Singapore Math® is a trademark of Singapore Math Inc.® and Marshall Cavendish Education Pte Ltd.

ISBN 978-0-358-10170-3

Printed in Singapore

2 3 4 5 6 7 8   1401   25 24 23 22 21 20
4500799762   B C D E F

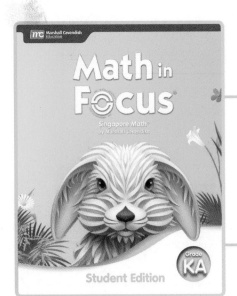

The cover image shows a lop-eared rabbit.
In the wild, rabbits come out at night to feed on grass.
The low light keeps them safe.
Rabbits like to chew on tough things like twigs, bark, and carrots.
This is because their teeth never stop growing!
They chew to keep their teeth short.